28/10/16

1 3 FEB 2017
2 6 MAR 2019

D0541712

For Tris, Audrey and Xavier – with all my love

With special thanks to Terry Bradley

Sharon Kaye is Professor of Philosophy at John Carroll University in Cleveland, Ohio. She graduated Phi Beta Kappa from the University of Wisconsin, Madison. After receiving her PhD in 1997 from the University of Toronto, she was a Killam postdoctoral fellow at Dalhousie University in Halifax, Nova Scotia. Since then, she has published numerous articles as well as books, including *Philosophy for Teens* Volumes I and II with Paul Thomson (2006, 2007), *Medieval Philosophy* (2008), *Black Market Truth*, Book One of The Aristotle Quest: A Dana McCarter Trilogy (2008), *Critical Thinking* (2009), *The Onion and Philosophy* (2010), *The Ultimate* Lost *and Philosophy* (2011), and *What Philosophy Can Tell You about Your Lover* (2012). Her works have been published in Japanese, Greek, Turkish, Spanish, Portuguese and Slovak.

Teach Yourself®

PHILOSOPHY
A complete introduction

Sharon Kaye

Contents

How to use this book

This book is arranged chronologically, with each chapter focused on a key philosopher whose ideas have challenged and enlarged philosophical thought in a significant way. Each begins with a thought experiment to introduce the reader to the crux of the philosopher's thought before moving on to an in-depth discussion of his ideas.

This Complete Introduction from Teach Yourself ® includes a number of special boxed features, which have been developed to help you understand the subject more quickly and remember it more effectively. Throughout the book you will find these indicated by the following icons:

 The book includes concise **quotes** from the philosopher under discussion in each chapter. They are referenced so that you can include them in essays if you are unable to get your hands on the source.

 The **case study** is a more in-depth introduction to a related topic. There is one in each chapter, and they should provide good material for essays and class discussions.

 The **key ideas** are highlighted towards the end of each chapter. If you have only half an hour to go before an exam, scanning through these would be a very good way of spending your time.

 The **fact-check** questions at the end of each chapter are designed to help you ensure that you have taken in the most important concepts from the chapter. If you find that you are consistently getting several answers wrong, it may be worth trying to read more slowly or taking notes as you go.

 The **spotlight** boxes offer interesting or amusing anecdotes to help bring the philosophers and their ideas to life.

 The **dig deeper** boxes give you ways to explore topics in greater depth than is possible in this introductory-level book.

Introduction

Philosophy is the most important subject you will ever study.

This may come as a surprise to you, since philosophers aren't very visible in our society. They don't have offices like lawyers or counsellors, where you go and pay a fee to receive a service. Nevertheless, they're everywhere. And it's a good thing, too, because society would collapse without them.

Philosophers are people who think about things. They stop and wonder why things are the way they are. They ask questions no one else has ever considered. They dream about how things might be different.

If you've ever done any of these things, then you're probably a philosopher. Perhaps just about everyone has had 'philosophical moments' from time to time. You can be a philosopher without any formal training. But – obviously – the more you know about philosophy the more philosophical you can be.

The best way to learn about philosophy is to study what great philosophers have said. That's exactly what philosphers did – they built upon their predecessors' ideas. The history of philosophy is the unfolding of an extraordinarily rich legacy of thought that has underpinned the development of Western civilization.

This book is designed to help you teach yourself philosophy. The goal is not just to teach yourself about philosophy, but to teach yourself to be a (better) philosopher. Why not? We need you. And, besides, it's fun.

This book will take a close look at 14 of the greatest philosophers who ever lived. We will examine their views, how they argued for them, and what their critics said about them.

Each philosopher is different. They ask different questions and have different concerns. They have very different ways of seeing the world. Yet they are all philosophers and they are united by three main themes, which you will see running throughout this book.

Theme 1: challenging authority

All the thinking that philosophers do results in some pretty radical ideas. It's not surprising, therefore, that philosophers often find themselves in deep trouble. Each of the philosophers we will meet in this book has his own tale of woe, which we can summarize as follows:

▶ Plato was sold into slavery for offending a tyrant.

▶ Aristotle was forced to abandon his school to avoid execution.

▶ Anselm was twice exiled for standing up to the king.

▶ Aquinas's use of Arabic philosophy was condemned by the pope.

▶ Descartes lived abroad without a permanent address for many years to escape the Inquisition.

▶ Hobbes was nearly murdered by royalists and pressured to burn his own works.

▶ Locke fled his homeland under suspicion of conspiracy.

▶ Hume was charged with heresy and blackballed from university teaching.

▶ Kant was reprimanded by the king and censored.

▶ Mill was arrested in 1823 at the age of 17 for distributing information about birth control and was denied admittance to Oxford and Cambridge for refusing to take Anglican orders.

▶ Nietzsche went insane.

▶ Wittgenstein wrote his most important work while serving in the trenches during World War I.

▶ Sartre was arrested for civil disobedience.

▶ Dewey forfeited his laboratory school over a conflict with the university administration.

There are many other great philosophers as well, and they often had even more tragic stories. Consider the case of the fifth-century-CE Roman woman Hypatia, who was stoned by an angry mob just for teaching philosophy.

It takes guts to be a philosopher. Although society needs philosophers, it also hates them. This is because philosophers provoke change. It's human nature to resist change.

If you were living in the fifth century CE, especially if you were a *woman* living in the fifth century CE, you might just decide to pass on philosophy. We couldn't blame you. But many brave men and women didn't pass. They refused to pass. And, thanks to them, you no longer have to worry about getting stoned … at least in most places around the world. You can pretty safely read this book and then go on to develop your own outrageously radical philosophy.

Theme 2: thought experiment

Philosophy is the mother of all the sciences. It existed before psychology, biology or chemistry. It gave birth to these fields of study by raising questions about the human mind, the human body and the nature of physical objects. When philosophers began investigating the world, they provided a foundation for all the knowledge we treasure today.

Although philosophy continues to push science in new directions, its methodology is not scientific. At the heart of science is experimental research: scientists conduct experiments in laboratories to gather data. Philosophers conduct experiments, too, but their experiments take place in the mind rather than in laboratories, and their goal is to explore possibilities rather than to collect data.

Philosophers call their research methodology **thought experiment**. A thought experiment is an imaginary scenario designed to test an idea. Here are a few examples:

1 Suppose you learn that invisible aliens are watching you. While not causing any harm, they follow you everywhere, hovering nearby while you sleep, listening to all your conversations, and seeing you naked. Do you mind? Why or why not? Are they doing anything wrong?

2 Suppose you learn that one of the people you interact with on a daily basis is actually a very sophisticated robot – but you are not told who it is. How would you figure it out? Are there some things humans can do that machines can't? Or are human beings actually a type of machine?

3 Suppose you thought you saw your friend Joe smoking cannabis at a concert. In fact, you did not see Joe, but someone else who happens to look like him. Nevertheless, Joe was at the concert smoking cannabis. Would it be correct to say that you knew the truth? Why or why not? What is required for a belief to be considered knowledge?

Various versions of these three thought experiments have been used to explore different areas of philosophy:

▶ The first concerns **ethics** – the study of right and wrong. Philosophers are interested in finding out whether morality can be rationally justified and whether there are any values that should apply to everyone regardless of how they feel about it.

▶ The second concerns **metaphysics** – the study of reality – which encompasses human nature as well as the nature of time, space and the universe itself. Philosophers are not convinced that things are always as they appear to be.

▶ The third concerns **epistemology** – the study of knowledge. We take it for granted that there is a difference between facts and opinions, but it is far more difficult than one might think to pinpoint that difference.

It is the business of philosophers to investigate ethics, metaphysics and epistemology. These areas are deeply connected and a complete philosophy would involve all three. The purpose of a thought experiment is to develop views in these areas and then to defend them against criticisms and alternative views.

Theme 3: no right answer

In addition to developing original ideas, philosophers spend a great deal of energy defending them. In fact, when it comes right down to it, philosophers love to argue. This might lead you to the impression that their goal is to convince the world that they are right.

This would be a mistaken impression, however. The purpose of philosophical argumentation is to find out whether or not a view is really true. A good philosopher would never want to win an argument for the sake of winning.

This makes philosophers different from lawyers. Lawyers aren't supposed to care whether their clients are guilty or innocent – because everyone deserves a fair trial regardless of the truth.

It also makes philosophers different from advertisers. Advertisers want everyone to believe that their product is the best, whether or not it really is. They try to convince you to buy their product whether or not you really want it or need it.

The whole goal of philosophy is to find the truth. Philosophers defend with all their hearts the views that they believe are true, and they want others to challenge them so that they can see whether they are right. Good philosophers are happy to modify or even abandon their views if their arguments don't hold up against criticism.

If you asked a group of people to answer the questions raised above in our three thought experiments, you would get a wide variety of answers. Part of the fun of philosophy is learning what other people think and sparring with them. As a philosopher, you will, of course, believe that your own views are true. But philosophy deals with questions that have not yet been answered, and so you have to recognize that others are perfectly entitled to disagree with you.

To say that philosophy deals with questions that have not yet been answered is not to say that its questions cannot be answered. People who are new to philosophy often find themselves wanting to say: 'There's no point in discussing philosophical questions because no one can ever know the answers!'

But this is an attitude that you have to move beyond. There is a lot of point to discussing philosophical questions:

▹ First, sometimes we actually do find the answers. Consider the fact that philosophers once wondered whether the world was round or flat. This question has now been answered! Today philosophers wonder whether time travel is possible. This question, like all philosophy questions, could one day be answered – even though it's hard for us in the present moment to see how.

- Second, sometimes the search for the answer is more important than the answer itself. Suppose you discovered that the answer to the meaning of life, the universe and everything is 42. This answer isn't going to make any sense until you better understand the question! Understanding the enduring questions human beings have been asking since the dawn of civilization is a big part of the search.

Philosophers are searching for the truth. It takes a community of inquirers, just like you, to make this a meaningful – and an ennobling – enterprise.

Enjoy the chapters to come!

> *There is a theory which states that if ever anyone discovers exactly what the Universe is for and why it is here, it will instantly disappear and be replaced by something even more bizarre and inexplicable.*
>
> *There is another theory which states that this has already happened.*
>
> Douglas Adams

Dig deeper

Kwame Anthony Appiah, *Thinking it Through: An Introduction to Contemporary Philosophy* (Oxford University Press, 2003).

Simon Blackburn, *Think: A Compelling Introduction to Philosophy* (Oxford University Press, 1999).

Thomas Cathcart and Daniel Klein, *Plato and a Platypus Walk into a Bar ... Understanding Philosophy through Jokes* (Penguin, 2008).

_____, *Aristotle and an Aardvark Go to Washington* (Abrams Image, 2008).

_____, *Heidegger and a Hippo Walk through Those Pearly Gates: Using Philosophy (and Jokes!) to Explore Life, Death, the Afterlife, and Everything in Between* (Viking, 2009).

1

Plato and justice

'Knowledge without justice ought to be called cunning rather than wisdom.'

Plato

In this chapter you will learn:

▶ *about the birth of philosophy with Plato's masterpiece* The Republic
▶ *why Plato made Socrates his hero*
▶ *the theory behind the Forms, Plato's most important thesis*
▶ *why Plato rejects realism in favour of idealism*
▶ *the meaning of the Allegory of the Cave*
▶ *how Plato answers the question 'What is justice?'*
▶ *about the role of love in the improvement of the soul.*

Thought experiment: the Ring of Gyges

You are on vacation on a remote Caribbean island enjoying a hike through the jungle by yourself. Exploring off the trail, you come to a small cave. On its floor lies a very old-looking golden ring in which is set a dark stone. Pleased with your discovery, you slip it on, planning to bring it home as a souvenir of your trip. As you continue your hike, however, you absent-mindedly spin the stone around your finger and an extraordinary thing happens: you become invisible!

Panicking for a moment, you spin the stone of the ring in the other direction and you magically reappear, unharmed. You test the ring a few times and try walking while invisible. Your footsteps appear in the mud, apparently by themselves. You pick up a stick and it fades out of sight; you put it down and it reappears.

Amazed with your discovery, your first thought is to run to the nearest town and show someone. As you enter the next clearing, however, you see an exquisite palace by the seashore. Expensive cars are pulling up, out of which spill men in tuxedoes and women in evening gowns. The surrounding gardens are crawling with security guards. Though instinct tells you to turn back quickly, you are very hot, tired and hungry. So you make yourself invisible and slip into the party.

After helping yourself to food from a sumptuous banquet table, you go upstairs to lie down for a while. Sitting on the bed of the first room you enter is a metal suitcase full of countless packets of $100 bills! The thought occurs to you: you could open an account at one of the notoriously discreet banks on the island and return home, set for life.

You start dreaming of all the things the ring could enable you to acquire. You could buy tickets to great concerts... scratch that – you could sit on stage with the performers! You could visit the homes of your favourite television heart-throbs - see what their lives are like, perhaps accompany them into the shower... You could punish your boss and your former lover in all kinds of interesting ways... You could get away with murder... You could do so many things. But what *should* you do? What *will* you do?

Do the right thing

The great ancient Greek philosopher Plato (c.428/427–c.348/347 BC) first presented a version of the Ring of Gyges thought experiment in his masterpiece, *The Republic*, which is today considered one of the greatest books of all time. It was the inspiration for J.R.R. Tolkien's epic novel *Lord of the Rings* as well as for many other great works of literature.

Like all of Plato's works, *The Republic* is a dialogue between characters who represent differing points of view. One of the characters in *The Republic* is Thrasymachus, who thinks it obvious that you should take the money and do all the things you've dreamed of. He goes so far as to insist that the thought experiment proves that the only reason people don't seize their own advantage in every situation is because they're afraid of getting caught. With the Ring of Gyges, you would never be caught, and so you would be a fool not to do exactly as you pleased.

The hero of *The Republic*, however, is Socrates (c.469–399 BC), who takes Thrasymachus to task, arguing that our hesitation about using the ring comes not only from our cowardice but also from our sense of justice. Stealing, cheating and murdering are wrong because they damage the community and they damage our own souls. The wise man seeks to be just in all his dealings even when he doesn't have to be.

Perhaps few would go along with Thrasymachus in rejecting justice altogether. But the Ring of Gyges raises the further question of what constitutes justice. When you thought about whether or not you would take the money, you probably considered the fact that it was most likely stolen or acquired illegally. You may have reasoned that this would make it fair game to steal. Likewise, maybe it would be OK to spy on a celebrity as long as they never knew about it. And it may actually be good to punish or even kill someone who really deserves it.

If you assembled a room full of people to discuss these questions, you would find a wide range of disagreement. One person might insist that the right thing would be to go to the police with the entire matter. Someone else might just as easily counter that neither the police nor any government can be trusted to do the right thing. After listening to all sides of the debate you're likely to conclude that there is no perfect solution, and you may be tempted to follow Thrasymachus, after all.

Plato (through his mouthpiece Socrates), however, finds a way to rescue justice. Impressed with the precision of mathematics, he asks us to consider the following analogy. Look all over the entire world and you will never find a perfect triangle. It is impossible enough to find a truly straight line, much less three that join at angles to make a plane figure. Yet everyone can picture a perfect triangle in their mind's eye. In fact, we use that image to judge the imperfectly triangular objects around us. Some are better instances than others. Though none are perfect, we can clearly identify which ones come closer to the ideal.

Plato argues that justice is similar – as are beauty, goodness and truth itself. We see only rough approximations around us. But we wouldn't be able to judge these approximations at all if there were no ultimate ideal with which to compare them. The job of the philosopher is to study and promote the ideal.

Case study: Socrates and the birth of philosophy

Plato was first in the history of Western civilization to publish philosophy. A talented wordsmith from an aristocratic family, he originally planned to become a playwright. But then, one day in Athens, he met a strange old fellow with bulgy eyes and a pug nose: Socrates.

No aristocrat himself, Socrates spent his days ambling through the marketplace barefoot, engaging people in conversation. He was searching for wisdom but was hard pressed to find any. He asked artists about beauty, teachers about truth, religious leaders about goodness, and lawyers about justice. No one was able to answer his penetrating questions.

In fact, Socrates so flustered the professionals of Athens that they began to resent him and wanted him to cease his disturbing inquiry. But it was too late. Socrates had already attracted a large body of young followers, who cheered him on. Eventually, a politician had him arrested for impiety and corrupting the city's youth.

At his trial, Socrates famously defended himself with a speech, comparing the state of Athens to a great and noble steed (i.e. a horse):

> 'The state is a great and noble steed who is tardy in his motions owing to his very size, and requires to be stirred into life. I am that gadfly that God has attached to the state, and all day long and in all places am always fastening upon you, arousing and persuading and reproaching you. You will not easily find another like me, and therefore I would advise you to spare me.'

> Plato, Apology 30e–31a, trans. Benjamin Jowett (http://classics. mit.edu/Plato/apology.html)

But the jurors voted not to spare him and he was sentenced to death by hemlock, a paralysing poison.

Socrates' devoted followers urged him to escape, which he could easily have done. Arguing, however, that he must respect the decision of his fellow citizens, Socrates fearlessly accepted his sentence.

In dying for his cause, Socrates became a martyr, setting a philosophical movement on fire. Plato founded the Academy, a school for *philosophy*, which term comes from the Greek words for 'love of wisdom'. There he would continue the inquiry that Socrates began on the streets of Athens. Plato's Academy is considered the first university, and it is the source of our modern term *academics*.

Immortalized as the hero of all of Plato's dialogues, Socrates is known as the founder of Western philosophy. It has often been said that the entire history of Western philosophy is but a footnote to Plato.

Spotlight

According to legend, Plato's birth name was Aristocles. His nickname, Plato, comes from the Greek word for 'broad'. It is disputed whether this was meant to refer to his mind or his body. According to the Monty Python 'Philosophers Song', 'Plato, they say, could stick it away; Half a crate of whisky every day.'

The Forms

The most important thesis in Plato's work, the thesis that shapes all his views, is that there are perfect exemplars of everything we imperfectly experience in this world (such as beauty, truth, goodness, justice and, of course, triangles). Plato reasons that these ideals must actually exist in a realm beyond our world of experience. If they existed only in our minds, they would be mere opinions, which would vary from person to person. In order for them to be objective and universal, they have to be real entities. Plato calls these entities **Forms**.

If the Forms exist beyond our world of experience, then how do we know about them? Plato answers this question by once again reflecting on mathematics. In his dialogue *Meno* Socrates asks a slave boy to solve a geometrical puzzle. The boy can't do it, of course, because he has never learned mathematics. But then Socrates breaks the puzzle down, asking the boy to tell him how to proceed each step of the way. The boy is amazed to discover that he can solve the puzzle, after all.

We have all experienced that wonderful 'Aha!' moment when we finally recognize the truth. It feels like seeing an old friend. Plato takes this feeling very seriously as evidence that the human soul once knew the Forms directly. Wisdom lies deep within our memories; we need only learn how to summon it. This is why the 'Socratic Method' is to teach by asking questions.

Spotlight

Socrates married a much younger woman named Xanthippe, who bore him three sons. But there was never a man less suited than Socrates for domestic life. He is reputed to have told his followers: 'By all means, marry. If you get a good wife, you'll be happy. If you get a bad one, you'll become a philosopher.'

Many Eastern religions teach the doctrine of the **transmigration of souls**, according to which the soul never really dies but passes from one bodily existence to the next. Plato, who spent some time studying Eastern thought, adapts this idea for his purpose.

The world around us is not 'true being' because it consists of constant change, which creates nothing but a succession of fleeting appearances. The wiser we become, the more we realize that true reality must exist in another, eternal realm. This realm is called **transcendent** because it is beyond our world.

Consider how you yourself have changed throughout your life – from baby, to child, to adult. Which of these is the real you? All of them? But that can't be because they have contradictory properties. For example, the child-you did not like coffee and the adult -you does. None of your physical selves is the real you, according to Plato. The real you is something constant within you, your soul, which cannot be seen with the bodily eye. Likewise, the Forms are invisible and unchanging. They are the eternal constants that unify our fragmented experience.

Idealism

The view that the material world around us is not real is called **idealism**. (Plato's particular version of it is sometimes called 'transcendental realism'.) It is directly opposed to **realism**, according to which the material world is real and knowable without transcendent Forms.

Plato rejects realism, insisting that it is incapable of securing objective and universal standards. If there are no Forms, he reasons, there is no way to evaluate competing opinions. Every opinion is equally valid. This result is called **relativism**.

Although relativism may sound acceptable or even appealing at first, upon closer examination it turns sour. If everyone's opinions are equal, then, for example, Hitler's opinions about justice are just as valid as Ghandi's and Mother Teresa's. But this implication is unacceptable – or at least deeply problematic! There must be some independent source of values. Idealism readily provides this.

The main complaint against idealism, on the other hand, is that it lacks scientific credibility. The transcendent realm, by definition, is beyond empirical measure. Why should we believe in something we cannot observe?

While idealism has opposed science at times throughout history, it has also supported science in surprising ways. After all, the scientific principles that underlie empirical investigation are not themselves observable. For example, Plato's conviction that the universe is modelled on perfect exemplars led him to hypothesize that the objects around us are constructed from invisible geometrical shapes (known as the Platonic solids). This hypothesis paved the way to modern chemistry.

The Allegory of the Cave

Regardless of whether or not you care to swallow the large metaphysical assumptions required for idealism, you may be sympathetic to the perspective it affords Plato. Seeing himself as a lover of wisdom, Plato is critical of the 'lovers of sights and sounds' who live life on a superficial level, never inquiring into the reality that lies beyond appearances. The mantra of his hero, Socrates, was: 'The unexamined life is not worth living.'

The only problem is that philosophical inquiry is a difficult undertaking. In *The Republic*, Plato tells a memorable story called the Allegory of the Cave to illustrate the problem.

Imagine yourself and a number of others in a cave chained to chairs facing the wall. There is a fire burning behind you and puppeteers are using the light from the fire to cast shadows on the wall in front of you. Because you have been here all your life, and these shadows are all you know, you assume that they are the sum total of reality.

One day, however, you break your chains and discover the source of the shadows. You climb out of the cave to make your escape. Daylight seems so bright by comparison to what you are used to that you can scarcely stand it at first. In time, you adjust and find life outside the cave breathtakingly beautiful.

Feeling bad for the other prisoners, you return to the cave to tell them that they are watching shadows from puppets which are modelled on creatures that live outside the cave. But they are content with their supposed reality and they don't want to follow you into the blinding light. In fact, they are angry with you for disturbing them and they think you have been corrupted, because you no longer appreciate or believe in the puppet show.

As a philosopher, Plato feels like the escaped prisoner. He has glimpsed the Forms, perfect exemplars of our everyday experiences, and wants to share his discovery. But most people just don't care. Although philosophy in general, and Platonic philosophy in particular, can sometimes seem abstract and even elitist, Plato shows that it is deeply motivated by a concern for securing the good life – for everyone.

The good life

The goal of Plato's *Republic* is to answer the question 'What is justice?' Proposing that justice in an individual person is parallel to justice in the state, Socrates sets out to describe an ideal city – a republic.

Plato's republic consists of three castes: the producers, the soldiers and the rulers (or 'guardians'). Through a universal education system, each citizen is assigned to the caste to which he or she is naturally fitted. To prevent the citizens from trying to change castes, the guardians propagate the myth that every human being is made of one of three metals. Those made of bronze are born to be producers, those made of silver are born to be soldiers, and those made of gold are born to be guardians.

Plato justifies this deception by virtue of its service to the greater good of the city, a strategy ever since dubbed the 'noble lie'.

To maintain order in the republic, the soldiers enforce the guardians' laws. Music, poetry and theatre, which promote the love of sights and sounds, are banned. The family unit is dissolved. The best men breed with the best women and the children are raised in a communal fashion. Those who show greatest promise in recollecting the Forms, whether male or female, become the philosopher-kings.

> *Until philosophers are kings, or the kings and princes of this world have the spirit and power of philosophy, and political greatness and wisdom meet in one, and those commoner natures who pursue either to the exclusion of the other are compelled to stand aside, cities will never have rest from their evils – no, nor the human race, as I believe – and then only will this our State have a possibility of life and behold the light of day.*
> Plato, *The Republic* V, 473c, trans. Benjamin Jowett (http://classics.mit. edu/Plato/republic.html)

In Plato's view, the only way to secure the good life for everyone is to restructure society as a whole.

Love

Just as the state must be properly ordered, so, too, must the individual soul. Metaphorically speaking, each one of us has a ruler, a soldier and a producer within us. In order to function well, we must ensure that each does its job and stays free of corrosive influences.

Plato famously describes the threefold structure of the soul through an analogy. The soul is like a chariot driven by two steeds. The charioteer represents reason (the ruler), one steed represents noble passions (the soldier), while the other represents base passions (the producer). The charioteer guides the chariot, trying to keep the horses from pulling in different directions.

Recall that Plato named himself, not a seeker or a finder, but a *lover* of wisdom. Love plays an important role in inspiring one towards the good life. We must fall in love with wisdom, and we can use our worldly experience with falling in love as a model. Plato writes poetically about how your lover can lead you to recollect the Forms:

> Now when the charioteer beholds the vision of love, and has his whole soul warmed through sense, and is full of the prickings and ticklings of desire, the obedient steed, then as always under the government of shame, refrains from leaping on the beloved; but the other, heedless of the pricks and of the blows of the whip, plunges and runs away, giving all manner of trouble to his companion and the charioteer, whom he forces to approach the beloved and to remember the joys of love. [...] And now they are at the spot and behold the flashing beauty of the beloved; which when the charioteer sees, his memory is carried to the true beauty, whom he beholds in company with Modesty like an image placed upon a holy pedestal. He sees her, but he is afraid and falls backwards in adoration, and by his fall is compelled to pull back the reins with such violence as to bring both the steeds on their haunches, the one willing and unresisting, the unruly one very unwilling.
>
> Plato, *Phaedrus*, trans. Benjamin Jowett (http://classics.mit.edu/Plato/phaedrus.html)

For Plato, the crucial point is that reason stays in control, taking you ever further away from this world into a state of perpetual spiritual connection with the transcendent realm. To this extent, Plato's philosophy has a strongly mystical side. Perhaps this is why so many elements of Platonism were incorporated into Christianity during its development in the Middle Ages.

Spotlight

The term 'platonic love' today refers to a strong, non-sexual bond. Plato recommended purely spiritual relationships as the highest form of love, though he also recommended starting with a lot of hot and sweaty gay sex.

Justice?

In *The Republic*, Plato undertakes to find out what justice is. Thrasymachus insists that there is no such thing as justice and Socrates sets out to prove him wrong. His investigation, however, brings him full circle – back to Thrasymachus, in a way. For he discovers that justice is a concept that arises only in dysfunctional circumstances. The ideal state, just like the ideal soul, is perfectly ordered. Therefore it has no need for justice. Obeying reason, everyone knows their place, and there is no conflict.

No wonder there are so many competing definitions of justice, and no wonder none of them is adequate. The very spectre of justice indicates deep structural flaws. Once proper order is established, questions about justice should no longer arise.

Plato's vision in *The Republic* is beautiful and yet also terrifying. On the one hand, it would be wonderful to live in an orderly society where everyone does as they should. On the other hand, achieving this order may require the most tyrannical of totalitarian regimes. In fact, totalitarian leaders such as Joseph Stalin have been greatly inspired by Plato. Plato's critics crystallize its greatest challenge in a single, disturbing question: Who will guard the guardians?

Key ideas

Allegory of the Cave: The story Plato tells to illustrate the difficulty of philosophical inquiry

Forms: Perfect exemplars of everything we imperfectly experience in this world

Idealism: The view that the material world around us is not real

Philosopher-kings: The rulers of Plato's republic

Realism: The view that the material world is real and knowable without recourse to transcendent Forms

Relativism: The view that every opinion is equally valid

Ring of Gyges: A mythical ring that makes you invisible

Fact-check

1 The Socratic Method is to teach by...
   a Example
   b Promise of reward
   c Threat of punishment
   d Asking questions

2 The word 'philosophy' comes from the Greek words for...
   a Reality, existence
   b Love, wisdom
   c Thought, experiment
   d Beauty, truth

3 Idealism is the view that true reality is...
   a Unknowable
   b Immaterial
   c Experiential
   d Unjust

4 How do we know the Forms exist, according to Plato?
   a We recollect them
   b We experience them
   c We create them
   d We acquire them

5 What does Plato call the eternal constants that unify our fragmented experience?
   a Forms
   b Experiments
   c Thoughts
   d Laws

6 What does Thrasymachus think the Ring of Gyges thought experiment proves?
   a That so-called justice is the fear of getting caught
   b That no one has the courage to challenge the law
   c That the government cannot be trusted
   d That only the material world is real

7 What does the Ring of Gyges do?
- **a** It makes you happy
- **b** It makes you invisible
- **c** It makes you rich
- **d** It makes you powerful

8 How does Plato propose to keep the citizens of his republic from changing caste?
- **a** By propagating a noble lie
- **b** By wielding an invincible police force
- **c** By keeping the other castes secret
- **d** By promising irresistible rewards

9 Why do the prisoners in Plato's Allegory of the Cave think the escapee is corrupted?
- **a** Because he tries to keep his escape a secret
- **b** Because he tells them a noble lie
- **c** Because he wants to put his chains back on
- **d** Because he no longer appreciates the puppet show

10 What do the two horses stand for in Plato's charioteer analogy?
- **a** The world around us and the transcendent realm
- **b** Just and unjust rulers
- **c** Noble and base passions
- **d** The individual and the state

Dig deeper

Thomas C. Brickhouse and Nicholas D. Smith, *Plato's Socrates* (Oxford University Press, 1994)

Russell Dancy, *Plato's Introduction of Forms* (Cambridge University Press, 2004)

Alfred Edward Taylor, *Plato: The Man and His Work* (Courier Dover Publications, 2001)

2

Aristotle and friendship

'A friend is a second self.'
Aristotle

In this chapter you will learn:

▶ *about Aristotle's doctrine of the four causes*

▶ *the meaning of teleology*

▶ *why not all friendships are equally valuable*

▶ *the doctrine of the golden mean*

▶ *how logic improves our reasoning*

▶ *how empiricists support their conclusions*

▶ *why Aristotle rejects Plato's idealism in favour of realism.*

Thought experiment: last wishes

You walk into a dimly lit room. Quiet music is playing. People are standing around in small groups, speaking in low voices with grave looks on their faces. You know a number of them; in fact, you know them all. It is surprising to see so many familiar faces, both relatives and friends, gathered in one place. They are wearing their nicest clothes, as are you. You look to the far end of the room. In the midst of several flower arrangements lies a casket.

Oh no, you think, someone I know has died. You walk reluctantly over to the casket and peer inside.

It's you!

'Hey!' you shout, moving towards the nearest group. No one turns to acknowledge you and you soon realize that they cannot see or hear you.

The music fades out and chimes sound. People begin shuffling into rows of chairs facing the casket. A man you don't recognize steps on to a podium. He thanks everyone for coming and announces that someone would now like to say a few words about the deceased.

You close your eyes in disbelief. Although half of you wants to run from the room, the other half wants to know what will be said.

Before you can decide what to do, the man introduces your best friend: the person who knew and loved you best. You freeze and can't help but listen. Your best friend begins by relating how you met. Then they tell some of the things you liked to do together and some of the things you accomplished together.

Hearing all of this makes you feel a warm glow inside.

After pausing for a sip of water, your best friend begins to tell a series of stories to illustrate the following:

▶ What made them look forward to seeing you

▶ What they admired most about you

▶ Why you were a good friend

- How you made their life, and the lives of others, better

- What they are going to miss most now that you are gone.

Your best friend stops, choking up a bit, and shuffles back into the audience.

While deeply honoured by the tribute, you also feel strangely disappointed. Are there some other accolades you know you did not earn but wish you had?

Seize the day

The ancient Greek philosopher Aristotle (384–322 BC) was Plato's most illustrious student. Although the philosophical dialogues he wrote do not survive, his last will and testament has. It paints a rare portrait of excellence. While modestly acknowledging his accomplishments, Aristotle shows tenderness and generosity towards his loved ones. It would be interesting to know what his best friend said about him at his funeral.

It's fitting that Aristotle achieved such excellence, considering that he spent a great deal of time thinking about how to attain it. Aristotle's ideas about the good life are recorded in a work known as the *Nicomachean Ethics*, which, like most of the works attributed to Aristotle, was probably a compilation of lecture notes. In it, Aristotle investigates the question of what makes for an excellent human being. He resists the temptation to make facile suggestions like those you might find in today's 'self-help' books. Ever the consummate philosopher, Aristotle grounds his investigation in metaphysics.

Spotlight

According to legend, Aristotle was the tutor of Alexander the Great, who went on to conquer the Persian Empire. Being infinitely interested in the exotic flora and fauna of the East, Aristotle is said to have asked Alexander to send him samples. One can only imagine the stench of the crates that would have arrived, having travelled up to 10,000 miles over tropical terrain.

The four causes

At the heart of Aristotle's metaphysics is the **doctrine of the four causes**, according to which true knowledge of something requires a fourfold explanation of its existence.

Suppose you are hosting some aliens from outer space, who are visiting earth for the first time. They have never seen a house before. 'What is a house?' they ask you. Aristotle would say that a proper explanation requires answering the following questions:

1 What is it made of? (the **material** cause)

2 Who made it? (the **efficient** cause)

3 What is its essence? (the **formal** cause)

4 Why does it exist? (the **final** cause)

The material cause of a house is the stone and wood from which it is made. Its efficient cause is the person who built it. Its final cause, or purpose, is to provide shelter. But what is the essence of a house?

The essence of a thing is its *sine qua non*, and it is closely related to its purpose. What features enable a house to provide shelter? They are not its particular colour or shape or size but, rather, the fact that it has four walls and a roof that enclose a space. Without enclosing space, a house would not be able to provide shelter – the wind and the rain would blow in. Enclosing space (in the manner planned out in the architect's drawing) is therefore the formal cause of the house.

Spotlight

Aristotle famously asserted that men have more teeth than women. His detractors have always found this quite hilarious because he claimed to base his science on observation, and anyone who actually bothered to count would see that men and women have exactly the same number of teeth. Recent studies, however, indicate that Aristotle may get the last laugh. It turns out that ancient Greek females routinely suffered from a vitamin deficiency that may have caused them to have fewer teeth.

Applying the doctrine of the four causes to the human being is surprisingly insightful. The material and efficient causes are easy – human beings are made of flesh and blood and made by their parents. But what are the formal and final causes of a human being?

Case study: the birth of science

Aristotle was a student-teacher at Plato's Academy when Plato died. Rather than taking over the Academy, Aristotle established his own school in Athens, called the Lyceum.

While the Academy was devoted to the abstract – even mystical – speculation that Plato had promoted, the Lyceum concerned itself with hands-on, scientific studies. Aristotle was insatiably curious about rocks, plants and animals. In fact, he collected specimens and made a careful study of their similarities, thereby inventing the species–genus classification system that became so important in the development of science.

Aristotle was also interested in the sky. Ancient Greek philosophers disprove the popular myth that, before Columbus discovered America, everyone believed the earth was flat. Plato speculated that the earth was round based on the idea that the circle is the perfect shape. If the divine maker of the earth is perfect, then he would certainly have made it the perfect shape. While rejecting Plato's mystical reasoning, Aristotle argued that the earth is round based on his observation of the lunar eclipse, in which the earth casts a curved shadow upon the moon.

Plato's mystical approach relies on controversial presuppositions – such as the notion of the divine and the notion of perfection. Plato considered these presuppositions justified on the grounds that they were born within (or innate to) the human mind, as discussed in the last chapter. Aristotle rejects these innate ideas, arguing instead that all knowledge comes from observation of the physical world around us. This view, which is the foundation of modern science, is known as **empiricism**.

Teleology

For Aristotle, the answer to this question of formal and final causes lies in **teleology**, the view that everything in the universe has a special function. For example, the function of oak trees is to produce acorns. An oak tree that fails to produce acorns is defective, and one that produces many good acorns is an excellent tree.

What do human beings contribute to the natural world? What makes us different from everything else in the universe?

Like rocks, we have mass. Like plants, we grow and reproduce. Like animals, we move ourselves around. But there is one thing we do that nothing else does – namely, we think. More specifically, we use our rational capacities to strive for happiness.

Ask anyone on the street what their ultimate goal is and they will be hard pressed to deny that everything they do is some small step in the quest for happiness. Aristotle's word for human happiness is **eudaimonia**, which literally means the state of having 'a good indwelling spirit', signifying a deeper sense of happiness than a dog or even a chimpanzee can achieve.

Aristotle famously defines the human being as the rational animal, making rationality our formal cause and happiness our final cause. The excellent human being is one who is good at reasoning about the good life.

Spotlight

An avid student of biology, Aristotle came to the carefully considered conclusion that the heart is the organ of thinking and the brain exists to cool the blood. Of course, it is true that the folded surface of the brain acts just like a radiator by increasing surface area. Aristotle was unwilling to perform lobotomies on prisoners, so how could he have known what the tiny cells on those surfaces were doing? Perhaps, though, we should all try harder to think with our hearts.

The golden mean

What constitutes good reasoning? Aristotle argued that, whenever we are faced with a situation that demands a choice, we should realize that there is a wide variety of possible responses, ranging from deficient through to excessive. The right response will always fall in the middle between those two extremes.

> *Both excessive and defective exercise destroys the strength ... while that which is proportionate both produces and increases and preserves it. So too is it, then, in the case of temperance and courage and the other virtues. For the man who flies from and fears everything and does not stand his ground against anything becomes a coward, and the man who fears nothing at all but goes to meet every danger becomes rash; and similarly the man who indulges in every pleasure and abstains from none becomes self-indulgent, while the man who shuns every pleasure, as boors do, becomes in a way insensible; temperance and courage, then, are destroyed by excess and defect, and preserved by the mean.*
>
> *Nicomachean Ethics*, Book II, Ch. 2 (http://classics.mit.edu/Aristotle/nicomachaen.2ii.html)

This is the **doctrine of the golden mean** – that the virtuous person avoids extremes, aiming always to act in a moderate fashion.

Consistent with his empirical approach, Aristotle would ask you to observe the people you admire most. Do they act in extreme ways? Extreme behaviour is often the result of emotional reactions. As rational animals, we are at our best when we use reason to control emotion and guide us towards a moderate response.

When you imagine your best friend speaking about you at your funeral, do you imagine them saying that you were level-headed during crises? That you knew just what to say or do to cheer them up? That you showed them how to have fun without getting into trouble? These are all examples of the Aristotelian golden mean. Clearly, there is much to be said for this doctrine.

At the same time, however, critics would point out that many of the people we admire most of all were extremists. Consider Ghandi, who starved himself to protest tyranny, or Mother Teresa, who devoted her entire life to helping the poor.

How would Aristotle respond to this objection? He might say that the apparent excess of these two was really only moderation, considering the extreme circumstances they faced. On the other hand, he might say that these two should not be admired so much after all. Either way, it is clear that there might be substantial disagreement over what constitutes the golden mean, and therefore that the doctrine needs further support.

Three types of friendship

The doctrine of the golden mean is supported by Aristotle's theory of friendship. Whereas Plato regarded justice as the highest good, Aristotle puts friendship above justice, pointing out that those who are friends have no need of justice while those who are just still need friends.

Aristotle is also famous for asserting: 'Without friends, no one would want to live, even if he had all other goods.' Does this seem true? Imagine yourself rich, famous and healthy, but completely friendless. Next imagine yourself poor, unhealthy and undistinguished, but surrounded by great friends. Which would you rather be? Obviously, you would rather have friends and other goods, but if you had to choose, wouldn't you choose friendship? Aristotle thinks you would.

Not all friendships are equally valuable, however. According to Aristotle, there are three different types.

The **friendship of utility** is a relationship you develop because it is mutually useful. You might have such a friendship with a co-worker or a neighbour. While you are working together or living nearby, you chat and help each other out. But the relationship does not keep you from changing jobs or moving away, and, once you do, you may never see the person again.

The **friendship of pleasure** is a relationship you pursue for mutual enjoyment. Aristotle has in mind individuals who get together to engage in a recreational activity. In this case, interest in the activity holds priority over the people involved. In a football team, for example, players may come and go without changing the game.

Both utility friendships and pleasure friendships are tenuous and probably temporary. They exist for the sake of something else. When in such a relationship, your love is directed primarily towards the utility or the pleasure and only incidentally towards the person who helps you achieve it.

The **friendship of virtue**, in contrast, is all about the people involved. Here, your love is directed primarily towards your friend and only incidentally towards whatever utility or pleasure they may help you achieve. This is the highest or most valuable form of friendship because, while it does not exclude utility or pleasure, it inspires the individuals to be good.

> *Perfect friendship is the friendship of men who are good, and alike in virtue; for these wish well alike to each other qua good, and they are good themselves. Now those who wish well to their friends for their sake are most truly friends; for they do this by reason of own nature and not incidentally; therefore their friendship lasts as long as they are good – and goodness is an enduring thing. And each is good without qualification and to his friend, for the good are both good without qualification and useful to each other. So too they are pleasant; for the good are pleasant both without qualification and to each other, since to each his own activities and others like them are pleasurable, and the actions of the good are the same or like. And such a friendship is as might be expected permanent, since there meet in it all the qualities that friends should have.*
>
> Nicomachean Ethics, Book VII, Part 3 (http://classics.mit.edu/Aristotle/nicomachaen.8viii.html)

A virtue friend is someone who cares about you for your own sake, thereby encouraging you to be the best person you can be. Because you care about them for their own sake, you want to be a good friend and do the things that will make them proud of you.

Aristotle asserted that true friends are like a single soul dwelling in two bodies, not so much because they are like-minded but because they provide a reflection for one another. Looking at a true friend is like facing a mirror: you see your own achievements and failures reflected back at you.

True friendship is rare. Although it does not come easily, it is something worth striving for. Aristotle was convinced that, in striving to be the best friend you can be, you have to exercise your rational capacities, and, in so doing, you learn to act in accordance with the golden mean.

Logic

Good reasoning is crucial, not only in the moral but also in the intellectual realm. This is why Aristotle became such an enthusiastic student of logic. In fact, he is considered the father of modern logic, insofar as he was the first to develop a systematic analysis of **deductive validity**.

Deductive validity is when the premises of an argument necessarily imply its conclusion. For example, consider the following argument:

1 Socrates is a man.

2 All men are mortal.

3 Therefore Socrates is mortal.

Steps 1 and 2 are the premises, that is, the reasons for the inference. Step 3 is the conclusion that is inferred. This is a good argument because the premises support the conclusion.

By way of contrast, consider the following argument:

1 Some geese are white.

2 Some chickens are white.

3 Therefore some crows are white.

Each of the premises is true. Nevertheless, it is not a good argument because the premises do not support the conclusion. Even if some geese and some chickens are white, there may not be any white crows. This is to say that the inference is not deductively valid.

The argument about Socrates, in contrast, is deductively valid because, if the premises are true, then the conclusion has to be true. We don't even need to know whether or not each of the steps is true in order to see that there is a necessary relationship between the premises and the conclusion.

It is very important to be able to recognize deductive validity because, if the structure of an argument is not valid, then there's no point in examining its content. When appraising a house, you must first make sure the floors will hold up before deciding whether or not you like the furniture!

A three-step argument like the one above about Socrates is called a **syllogism**. As it turns out, you can create 24 different types of syllogism by using the following four formulas (where the variables 'A' and 'B' could stand for anything you like):

1 All As are B.

2 Some As are B.

3 No As are B.

4 Some As are not B.

Not all syllogisms are deductively valid, however. Aristotle carefully laid them out and sorted them, discussing problematic inferences. By introducing this sort of logical analysis, he set a rigorous standard for intellectual debate for ever after.

Realism

The greatest debate between Plato and Aristotle, which has become a central point of controversy among philosophers ever since, concerns the Forms. As we saw in Chapter 1, Plato argued that knowledge depends on ideal exemplars existing beyond our world. If there are no objective and universal Forms to judge our ideas against, then we are left with nothing but opinions.

Aristotle denies that Plato's ideal exemplars exist. As an empiricist, he refuses to believe in anything that can't be experienced first hand. He brings Plato's Forms down to earth by asserting that they are really just the 'sensible forms' of things, which can be observed through the five senses.

> By a 'sense' is meant what has the power of receiving into itself the sensible forms of things without the matter. This must be conceived of as taking place in the way in which a piece of wax takes on the impress of a signet-ring without the iron or gold; we say that what produces the impression is a signet of bronze or gold, but its particular metallic constitution makes no difference: in a similar way the sense is affected by what is coloured or flavoured or sounding, but it is indifferent to what in each case the substance is; what alone matters is what quality it has.
>
> Aristotle, *De Anima*, Book II, Ch.12 (http://www.aquinasonline.com/Magee/da2-512htm)

When you see a purple onion, you can notice the purpleness it has in common with other purple objects. This means abstracting its colour away from its substance. You can think about purpleness all by itself, independently of any material object. But this does not mean that purpleness really exists in a transcendent realm beyond our world. It exists as a concept in our minds.

For Aristotle, the same holds for justice, and beauty, and truth itself. In his view, to say that these are concepts we abstract from the world is not to reduce them to mere opinions. Someone who called a purple onion 'green' would be incorrect, and there might be something wrong with his vision. Likewise, someone who called an unjust action 'just' would be incorrect, and there might be something wrong with his moral sense.

Aristotle is a realist, because he affirms that the material world is real and knowable without transcendent Forms. His view is also sometimes called **immanent realism**, insofar as it asserts that the forms required for knowledge reside within the objects we perceive rather than in a transcendent realm.

But can Aristotle succeed with the comparison between purple and justice? Critics may insist that moral qualities, like justice, are so unlike physical qualities, like purple, that they cannot be perceived through the five senses. Aristotle, and any empiricist like him, will have to work hard to prove that our perceptions can yield true knowledge of the world around us.

Key ideas

Deductive validity: Where the premises of an argument necessarily imply its conclusion

Doctrine of the four causes: True knowledge of something requires a fourfold explanation of its existence

Doctrine of the golden mean: The virtuous person avoids extremes, aiming always to act in a moderate fashion

Empiricism: Knowledge comes from observation of the physical world around us – the foundation of modern science

Friendship of pleasure: A relationship you pursue for mutual enjoyment

Friendship of utility: A relationship you develop because it is mutually useful

Friendship of virtue: A relationship in which your love is directed primarily towards your friend and only incidentally towards whatever utility or pleasure they may help you achieve

Syllogism: A three-step argument

Teleology: The view that everything in the universe has a special function

Fact-check

1 Aristotle argues that the formal cause of the human being is...
- **a** To find happiness
- **b** Having the essence of a rational animal
- **c** Virtue
- **d** Flesh and blood

2 If an argument is deductively valid, then the inference is...
- **a** Probable
- **b** Inadequate
- **c** Necessary
- **d** Arbitrary

3 Which of the following is the highest form of friendship, according to Aristotle?
- **a** Pleasure
- **b** Utility
- **c** Knowledge
- **d** Virtue

4 Aristotle argues that being virtuous means acting in which of the following ways?
- **a** Moderately
- **b** Extremely
- **c** Predictably
- **d** Usefully

5 How is the colour purple like justice, in Aristotle's view?
- **a** Both are Forms in a transcendent realm
- **b** Both can be perceived through the five senses
- **c** Both are ultimately illusions
- **d** Both are formal causes of physical objects

6 Which of the following studies would appeal to an empiricist?
- **a** Dissecting animals
- **b** Meditating
- **c** Reading other studies
- **d** Applying universal laws

7 Which of the following best describes the following argument?
1. The first goose flew south
2. The second goose flew south.
3. The third goose flew south.
4. Therefore, the fourth goose will fly south.
   a Invalid
   b Deductive
   c Syllogism
   d Necessary

8 In a friendship of virtue, each values the other...
   a As a means of achieving virtue
   b Because they are useful
   c As long as they enjoy the same activities
   d For their own sake

9 Aristotle is called a 'realist' because...
   a He was practical
   b He believed the Forms are real
   c He rejected visionary politics
   d He affirmed that the material world around us is real and knowable

9 Which of the following would Aristotle find most praiseworthy?
   a Saving as much money as you can
   b Training to break an Olympic record
   c Staying up all night to do well in an exam
   d Attending the wedding of an old friend

Dig deeper

J. Lear, *Aristotle: The Desire to Understand* (Cambridge University Press, 1988)

C.D.C. Reeve, *Substantial Knowledge: Aristotle's Metaphysics* (Hackett, 2000)

C. Shields, *Aristotle* (Routledge, 2007)

3

Anselm and God as supreme being

'Faith seeks understanding.'
Anselm of Canterbury

In this chapter you will learn:

▶ *the meaning of Pascal's Wager*
▶ *about Anselm's attempt to prove the existence of God*
▶ *why Gaunilo and others reject the proof*
▶ *the problem of evil*
▶ *the meaning of theodicy*
▶ *how Augustine argues that evil is necessary*
▶ *why atheists think evil disproves the existence of God.*

Thought experiment: the greatest gamble

You wake up in a blurry, unfamiliar room. You are lying in a bed with white covers. You cannot move. Your head is throbbing.

There is a woman in the room. She checks a machine by your bed and tells you that you're in hospital. As she speaks, the room grows brighter and brighter. The light is coming from above you. Its source is unfathomably warm and beautiful. It speaks to you: 'I will give you eternal life, if only you believe in me.'

You wake up again in the same bed in the same room. Your head is no longer throbbing and you can move freely. You soon learn that you have made a miraculous recovery from a serious car accident.

After leaving the hospital, you cannot stop thinking about your encounter with the bright light. Sometimes you feel sure it was God. At other times you feel it was just a dream induced by your head injury.

What should you believe?

At last you tell a friend about it. He responds as follows.

There are two possibilities: either it was God or it was not God. And you have two choices: to believe or not to believe. Combining the two possibilities with your two choices yields four possible results:

1. If it was God and you choose to believe, then you will receive an infinitely valuable reward – eternal life.

2. If it was God and you choose not to believe, then you will lose eternal life – in effect, an infinite penalty.

3. Suppose it was not God and you choose to believe. What have you lost? Nothing. You suffer only the disappointment of being wrong.

4. Suppose it was not God and you choose not to believe. What have you gained? Only the satisfaction of being right.

So, essentially, you are embarked on a great gamble, the greatest gamble of all. No matter how unclear your encounter may have been, the best course of action is clear. You have everything to gain and nothing to lose by believing.

In fact, when you think of it this way, no one can afford not to believe in God. Regardless of whether or not you have ever had an 'encounter', the fact that there could be a God who will give eternal life to those and only those who believe should be enough to motivate your belief. A finite sacrifice for a chance at infinity – right?

The Age of Faith

After the death of Aristotle, intellectual activity in Europe slowly sank into a steep decline. The Roman Empire rose and then fell, leaving chaos in its wake. The long, dark medieval period, or 'Middle Ages', arrived, lasting from about AD 400 to 1400.

Life was tough during the medieval period. You counted it a good day if you simply survived. Most people never even learned to read, much less studied philosophy. With few exceptions, the Church alone kept education alive. If you were lucky enough to be born with good brains, your best bet was to join a monastery as soon as possible.

It's not surprising, therefore, that the few philosophers the medieval period managed to produce were theologians, preoccupied with theories about God. In this unscientific era, miracles seemed to happen every day and plenty of people were convinced that they had experienced God directly. Nor was it socially acceptable to question God's existence.

But can God's existence be proven? This was a challenge medieval intellectuals felt ready to tackle. Some maintained that belief in God was a matter of faith alone, while others insisted that there are convincing arguments to support faith.

In Chapters 1 and 2 we saw how Plato and Aristotle pioneered two opposing **epistemologies,** or approaches to the search for knowledge. Plato's epistemology, based on innate principles, is abstract and mystical; Aristotle's, based on sensory experience of the world, is concrete and empirical. The debate between them persisted through the medieval period, garnering followers on both sides and creating divergent approaches to theology.

Anselm of Canterbury (1033–1109) makes an argument for the existence of God inspired by Plato's innatist approach.

Case study: Blaise Pascal and fideism

Considering how difficult it is to prove the existence of God, it's not surprising that many philosophers have argued that theism is a matter of faith alone.

The thought experiment at the beginning of this chapter is based on a legend concerning the French philosopher Blaise Pascal (1623–62). Pascal was a child prodigy who scorned religion until he was involved in a carriage accident that nearly cost him his life. He experienced a revelation, joined a church, and was left with the awkward task of explaining his change of heart to his sceptical friends. The result was 'Pascal's Wager' – the gamble for eternal life.

The view that we should believe in God without proof is known as **fideism**, from the Latin word for 'faith'.

Of course, there are significant problems with Pascal's Wager. Suppose that, based on your supernatural experience in hospital, you decide to believe in God. Then, that very night, you have another supernatural experience. This time, you hear a different voice saying it will condemn you to an eternity in hell if you believe the first voice!

Now what? Which voice should you believe?

Once you make up your mind which voice to believe, we'll just add a third voice, and then a fourth, and so on. Before you know it, you'll be ready for the loony bin.

While few people experience a supernatural conflict like this, the very possibility of such a conflict calls into question the idea of believing in order to earn a reward. That is, if you reason 'I guess I should go to church and pray, just in case there is a powerful being who wants me to,' you can just as easily reason 'I guess shouldn't go to church and pray, just in case there is a powerful being who doesn't want me to.' What makes one line of reasoning any better than the other?

Another criticism of Pascal's Wager comes from the American philosopher William James (1842–1910), who argues that it provides the wrong kind of motivation for sincere religious belief. He doubts that any God would look kindly on someone who believes in order to gain eternal life. James writes:

> 'We feel that a faith in masses and holy water adopted wilfully after such a mechanical calculation would lack the inner soul of faith's reality; and if we were ourselves in the place of the Deity, we should probably take particular pleasure in cutting off believers of this pattern from their infinite reward.'
>
> William James, *The Will to Believe and Other Essays in Popular Philosophy* (http://www.gutenberg.org/files/26659/26659txt)

The ontological proof

Anselm was a Benedictine monk who became archbishop of Canterbury. He describes his entire philosophy as 'faith seeking understanding', insisting that he himself never felt he needed proof of the existence of God. His excuse for developing a proof comes from a Bible passage concerning a 'fool who hath said in his heart that there is no God'. Anselm's ingenious proof is addressed to this 'fool' – an atheist, someone who does not believe in God.

The proof is called 'ontological' from the Greek word for 'being' because it is based on a distinction between two different kinds of existence: mental and real. A painting provides a good example of this distinction: first it exists in the mind of the artist, and then, after the artist creates it, it exists in reality.

The issue between the theist and the atheist, according to Anselm, is whether God exists only in the mind or whether he exists both in the mind and also in reality. Each side of the debate should agree that God exists in the mind. After all, even the most die-hard atheists can think of God; if they couldn't, then they wouldn't understand what they didn't believe in. Therefore, God certainly has 'being-in-the-mind'.

But there are plenty of things that have 'being-in-the-mind' without having 'being-in-reality'. Consider Santa Claus.

Everyone knows who Santa Claus is. Close your eyes for a moment right now and think about Santa... You know just how Santa looks (the red suit, the white beard, the twinkle in his eye), and you know all sorts of things about him (the workshop at the North Pole, the sleigh led by Rudolf, the Christmas Eve gift deliveries). Yet (spoiler alert!) you also know that he doesn't exist.

You might be thinking that, as long as you have an idea of God in your own mind, then he exists for you, regardless. But this is a confusion. After all, little children around the world have an idea of Santa in their own minds. This doesn't mean that Santa exists for them. It means that they think he exists. And, of course, they're wrong about that, as they will soon find out.

Now compare the case of Santa Claus to the case of Johnny Depp. Everyone knows who he is, too. Close your eyes and think about him right now...

You know what he looks like and you know all sorts of things about him. What's more, if you could find his house and get him to answer his door, you could actually meet him. This is to say that Johnny Depp has 'being-in-the-mind' as well as 'being-in-reality'.

Anselm's question is this: Is God like Santa or is God like Johnny Depp?

Spotlight

Two goldfish in a bowl talking:

Goldfish 1: Do you believe in God?

Goldfish 2: Of course I do! Who do you think changes the water?

Defining God

The atheist argues that God is like Santa: everyone is going to find out some day that he doesn't really exist. But can God have being-in-the-mind while lacking being-in-reality, as the atheist supposes? Anselm thinks not. In order to understand why, we must look closer at God's being-in-the-mind.

When we think of God, what do we think of? God is supposed to be the supreme being of the universe. At the very least, he is all-loving, all-knowing, all-powerful and eternal. No doubt he has a great number of other characteristics, some of which we may not be able to imagine. One thing we can say for certain, however, is that God is that being than which no greater can be conceived. If you can think of a being that is greater than God, then you don't understand what God is.

So, Anselm proposes that the theist and the atheist should agree to define God as that being than which no greater can be conceived. Admittedly, the grammar of this definition is a little awkward. For simplicity, we could substitute 'greatest conceivable being'. But this would presuppose that the human mind can fully conceive of God, which may not be the case. Although we may not be able to fully conceive of God, we at least know that we can't conceive of anything greater than God. Hence, the theist and the atheist should agree that this is how God exists in the mind: as that being than which no greater can be conceived.

Once atheists grant this step, however, the rest of the argument comes crashing down on them with alarming speed. Observe Anselm's irresistible logic:

> *Hence, even the fool is convinced that something exists in the understanding, at least, than which nothing greater can be conceived. For, when he hears of this, he understands it. And whatever is understood, exists in the understanding. And assuredly that, than which nothing greater can be conceived, cannot exist in the understanding alone. For, suppose it exists in the understanding alone: then it can be conceived to exist in reality; which is greater.*
>
> Anselm, *Proslogium* (www.fordham.edu/halsall/basis/anselm-proslogium.asp)

Existing in reality and in the mind is greater than existing in the mind alone. So, if God existed only in the mind, then it would be possible to conceive of a being that is greater than him. But it is impossible for there to be a being that is greater than the greatest being! This is a contradiction in terms. Therefore God must not exist only in the mind. He must exist both in the mind and in reality.

Gaunilo's response

Anselm's argument is still today considered one of the cleverest ever made. It has received a great deal of attention from philosophers of every stripe throughout history. So compact and powerful – it should make everyone think twice.

Nevertheless, it is not foolproof. In fact, another monk named Gaunilo of Marmoutiers wrote a reply to Anselm 'on behalf of the fool'. In it, Guanillo points out that, if Anselm's argument works for God, then it should work for a whole host of other beings that are completely imaginary.

For example, think of 'Lost Island' – that island than which no greater can be conceived. Surely this island must really exist, because, if it didn't have being-in-reality as well as being-in-the-mind, then it would be possible to conceive of an island that was greater than that island than which no greater can be conceived. Impossible! So Lost Island exists… along with the Best Mango, the Perfect Car, the Ideal Lover, and whatever else you like – which is absurd.

Guanilo's argument is a parody of Anselm's reasoning, indicating that something has gone dreadfully wrong. But it's not easy to put one's finger on the exact problem.

Two kinds of existence?

Perhaps the problem lies in Anselm's twofold conception of existence. Anselm sets out to prove that God has being-in-reality in addition to being-in-the-mind – as though being-in-reality and being-in-the-mind are two different ways for something to exist. But, on closer examination, this is a strange proposal.

When you say 'Santa Claus exists in my mind', what you really mean is 'I have an idea of Santa.' And having an idea of something doesn't necessarily mean that thing has mental existence.

Consider what happens in your brain when you think of Santa – certain neurons fire. It's not as though a little guy in a red suit literally pops into your head. It may *feel* like that, especially if you have a vivid imagination – it feels as though you can 'see' Santa in your mind. But a thought is actually an action – it's a tiny motion in your brain; it's not a *thing* at all.

If there is no such thing as 'being-in-the-mind', then Anselm's proof cannot get off the ground.

Of course, idealists insist that the physical world is not ultimately real. If Plato is right, then the apparent actions in our brains really are reflections of an eternal realm of Forms. Perhaps these Forms have being-in-the-mind, entitling Anselm to his twofold conception of existence, after all.

In the end, whether or not you are sympathetic to the ontological proof largely depends on your epistemology. Empiricists reject Anselm's approach on the grounds that it posits a kind of being that is not empirically observable. Meanwhile, many innatists insist that Anselm's argument actually works and is completely convincing.

Whether or not the ontological proof works, its concept of God as 'that being than which no greater can be conceived' highlights an important philosophical problem.

The problem of evil

In ancient times, before the rise of Christianity in Europe, the dominant religion was polytheism – belief in many gods. One of the great advantages of polytheism is that it enables you to explain why the world is so full of sorrow: the gods often fight among themselves and, when they do, human beings pay the price.

War, disease, death, destruction, hunger, filth, poverty, torture, crime, corruption, the Ice Capades... This is not good work. If this is the best God can do, I am not impressed. Results like these do not belong on the résumé of a Supreme Being.

George Carlin

In the Middle Ages, polytheism was replaced by monotheism – belief in a single, supreme God, which Anselm so famously defined. While simplifying faith, belief in one God makes our sorrowful world hard to understand. If God is 'that being than which no greater can be conceived', then why is his creation so full of trouble?

This question was especially vivid during the European Middle Ages when even basic survival was so hard. War, famine, plague, bitter cold, poor sanitation, abject poverty and rampant crime made life almost unbearable for the vast majority of people – and the situation is similar today in many places around the world. It may be understandable for God to punish bad people by letting them suffer. But why do bad things happen to good people? This is known as **the problem of evil**.

If something especially tragic has ever happened to you, you may have pondered the problem of evil yourself. For some, the inordinate amount of suffering in this world provides proof against the existence of God. In fact, the problem of evil is probably the most influential argument for atheism. Philosophers make the argument this way:

1 If God exists, then he is all-knowing, all-powerful and all-loving.

2 If God is all-knowing, then he knows about all the evil in the world.

3 If God is all-powerful, then he is able to banish it.

4 If God is all-loving, then he wants to banish it.

5 Yet evil has not been banished.

6 Therefore, God must not exist.

Defence of God

Of course, theists have presented many possible responses to this argument. A defence against the charge that evil is inconsistent with God's existence is known as a **theodicy**. Theodicies usually attack step 4 of the above argument, saying that, although God is all-loving, he doesn't want to banish all the evil in the world. On the contrary, he has good reasons for allowing it.

The Roman Christian philosopher Augustine of Hippo (354–430 CE), who was greatly influenced by Plato and a great influence upon Anselm, was deeply concerned about the problem of evil.

At first, Augustine thought that God allowed evil in the world in order to protect human free will. If God prevented us all from making bad choices, then we would be robots rather than human beings. Augustine soon realized, however, that this explanation cannot account for natural evils, such as birth defects, tornados or random accidents, which don't involve bad choices.

In order to account for natural evils, Augustine developed the idea that the goodness comes in degrees.

> And in the universe, even that which is called evil, when it is regulated and put in its own place, only enhances our admiration of the good; for we enjoy and value the good more when we compare it with the evil. For the Almighty God, who, as even the heathen acknowledge, has supreme power over all things, being Himself supremely good, would never permit the existence of anything evil among His works, if He were not so omnipotent and good that He can bring good even out of evil. For what is that which we call evil but the absence of good?
>
> Augustine, *Enchiridion*, Ch. 11 (http://www.leaderu.com/cyber/books/augenchiridion/enchiridion01-23html)

In this passage, Augustine asserts that evil is necessary in order to appreciate goodness. If God had made a perfect world, human beings would take it for granted – like a bunch of spoiled rich kids.

The main problem with this argument is that it doesn't account for the unequal distribution of evil. Think of a child born in Africa with sickle cell anaemia. She is sick from the day she is born, grows up in poverty, never learns to read, and dies before reaching adulthood. Another child born as healthy as can be in Canada has loving parents, laughs and plays happily every day of her life, receives an excellent education, marries well and raises a beautiful family. This seems extremely unfair. If a mother treated her own two children in such an unequal way, we would declare her unfit for motherhood. Yet God is supposed to be the wisest parent of all.

Augustine considered this problem and concluded that God must store up special rewards in heaven for those who experience undue suffering during life on earth. Maybe we should feel sorry for the Canadian child instead, because her happiness is only temporary.

This is an interesting proposal. Would it be acceptable for a mother to shower one of her children with benefits while allowing the other to suffer, provided she later gave a special reward to the one who suffered? Which child would you rather be: the child who neither suffers nor receives the special reward or the one who suffers and then receives the special reward? Should one be given a choice in the matter?

These are rather outrageous questions – questions that some religious believers would regard as inappropriate. According to tradition, it is not for human beings to question God's mysterious ways. But, according to philosophers, there is no such thing as an inappropriate question. It's no wonder they're always getting into trouble.

Key ideas

Atheist: Someone who does not believe in God

Epistemology: An approach to the search for knowledge

Fideism: The view that we should believe in God without proof

Monotheism: Belief in a single, supreme God

Ontological proof: Anselm's argument for the existence of God based on a distinction between two different kinds of existence: mental and real

Pascal's Wager: The gamble for eternal life: you have everything to gain and nothing to lose by believing in God without proof

Polytheism: Belief in many gods

Problem of evil: Why do bad things happen to good people?

That being than which no greater can be conceived: Anselm's definition of God

Theodicy: A defence against the charge that evil is inconsistent with God's existence

Fact-check

1 The view that we should believe in God without proof is known as…
- **a** Epistemology
- **b** Teleology
- **c** Ontology
- **d** Fideism

2 Which of the following provides a criticism of Pascal's Wager?
- **a** The Easter Bunny could give an eternal reward to all and only those who believe in him
- **b** One should have a choice about whether or not to believe in God
- **c** Everyone has the right to believe what they want
- **d** The world is not ultimately real

3 Anselm's ontological proof of the existence of God is based on which of the following?
- **a** A distinction between two different kinds of existence
- **b** The design we observe in nature
- **c** A gamble for an infinite reward
- **d** The problem of evil

4 Which of the following is an epistemological question?
- **a** Why do bad things happen to good people?
- **b** Why is the universe just right for life?
- **c** Does God have or lack being?
- **d** Can the existence of God be proven?

5 Guanilo's critique of Anselm's ontological proof is which of the following?
- **a** A contradiction
- **b** A parody
- **c** A wager
- **d** A theodicy

6 Anselm is which of the following?
- **a** An innatist
- **b** An empiricist
- **c** A fideist
- **d** A polytheist

7 Anselm argues that God must exist in reality because otherwise...
   a   Human beings could never have thought of him
   b   It would be possible to conceive of a being greater than him
   c   Human beings would despair in times of great suffering
   d   There would be no infinite reward

8 How many kinds of being do you have, according to Anselm?
   a   One
   b   Two
   c   Three
   d   Four

9 Which of the following is a criticism of the ontological proof?
   a   The distribution of evil in the world is unfair
   b   The world might not have a beginning
   c   Thoughts are not beings
   d   God does not look kindly on gambling

10 Which of the following is the best metaphor for Augustine's theodicy?
   a   Although candy tastes good, it isn't good for you
   b   You have to climb up the ladder before you can slide down the slide
   c   A painting must have dark patches in order to highlight the bright patches
   d   Fossils prove that dinosaurs once existed

Dig deeper

Katherine Rogers, *The Anselmian Approach to God and Creation* (Edwin Mellen Press, 1997)

Alvin Plantinga, *The Ontological Argument, from St. Anselm to Contemporary Philosophers* (Anchor Books, 1965)

Thomas Williams and Sandra Visser, *Anselm*, Great Medieval Thinkers (Oxford University Press, 2009)

Aquinas and God as cosmic creator

'Poets and philosophers are alike in being big with wonder.'

Thomas Aquinas

In this chapter you will learn:

- ▶ *the difference between a priori and a posteriori arguments*
- ▶ *how Boethius reconciles human freedom with God's foreknowledge*
- ▶ *how Aquinas uses motion to argue for the existence of God*
- ▶ *the meaning of brute fact*
- ▶ *how Aquinas uses purpose to argue for the existence of God*
- ▶ *how evolution accounts for the appearance of purpose*
- ▶ *the significance of the anthropic principle.*

Thought experiment: the view from eternity

Your life has been steadily improving over the last year. You've sorted out your relationships, you've secured the job of your dreams, and now you've won a trip to an exotic island paradise on the other side of the world.

You can hardly believe how fortunate you are during your first day there until, just before nightfall, disaster strikes.

You're just sitting down to a sumptuous meal when you hear a disturbance at the door. It's the police. They force their way in, scan the crowd and head straight for you. After muttering a few words to you in a language you don't understand, they haul you away and throw you into a dark, dank prison cell.

Days pass. You have contact only with two guards, who don't speak to you. At last, another prisoner is thrown into your cell. He explains the situation to you in stilted English. An insanely paranoid dictator has taken over the island. Arresting all foreigners on charges of espionage, he whimsically executes about half of them and lets the other half go. Your case will be decided tomorrow.

You are terrified. That night you have a vivid dream in which a woman in a long robe decorated with Greek letters appears to you. Introducing herself as 'Lady Philosophy', she tells you not to worry. There is a God in heaven who knows exactly what's going on. The future will unfold exactly according to his plan, which will be best for everyone.

Although you want to believe her, you see a problem.

'This dictator is going to decide by his own free choice whether I live or die tomorrow,' you object. 'He could go either way according to his whim at the moment. So no one can know what he will decide. Or, if someone can know what he will decide, then he isn't really free to go either way after all.'

Lady Philosophy shakes her head. 'Someone who knows how the future will go does not cause the future to go that way,' she insists. 'Suppose I study the weather and accurately predict a tornado. I didn't cause that tornado to occur.'

You shake your head in return. 'I'm not saying God would cause the dictator's choice; I'm saying he would guarantee it. Your prediction wouldn't guarantee the tornado, because you could be wrong. But God can't be wrong. Whatever he says will happen has to happen.'

Lady Philosophy nods. 'What you're saying would be true if God saw events before they happened. But God is eternal. This means he lives outside our timeline. He doesn't have to wait for things to happen. He experiences all of time at once.'

'What? How can that be?' you ask.

'God is like a man on a mountaintop watching a caravan on the road far below. In one glance, he sees the beginning, the middle and the end of the caravan. The caravan is like the past, the present and the future. To him, there is no distinction. But to us there is. Because we live in time, we have to experience events in succession, just like someone watching the caravan go by from the side of the road.'

'So, you're saying that, for God, tomorrow is already happening?'

'Tomorrow, today and yesterday always have been and always will be. The passage of time is a human illusion.' Lady Philosophy began to flicker a little as the dream drew to a close.

You turn over in your sleep, wondering whether you can trust an illusion for the truth about an illusion.

The consolation of philosophy

As the Middle Ages progressed, philosophers developed a growing interest in cosmology – an account of the nature of the universe. Accordingly, they began to turn away from Plato's innatist approach towards Aristotle's empiricist approach.

Aristotle's works, which had been lost during the early medieval period, became available towards the end of the period, as universities were founded in major cities such as Paris and Oxford. One of the most avid readers of Aristotle during this time was the Italian philosopher Thomas Aquinas (1225–74). Though Aristotle was a pre-Christian thinker, Aquinas wanted to use his ideas to support and defend all the major tenets of the Christian faith, starting with the existence of God.

Spotlight

Thomas Aquinas's nickname as a postgraduate was 'The Dumb Ox', simply because the poor man had gone off to study in Cologne without knowing any German. This is rather ironic, considering that he went on to make an encyclopedic contribution to philosophy and is regarded as one of the most influential thinkers of all time.

Anselm's ontological proof of God, which we examined in the last chapter, is called **a priori**, meaning that it is 'prior to', or independent of, experience of the world. As a follower of Plato, Anselm relies on innate ideas and reason alone to make his case.

Rejecting Anselm's proof as unsound, Aquinas famously presents five **a posteriori** arguments for the existence of God, all of which are 'after', or dependent upon, experience of the world. The first and the fourth of the 'Five Ways' are the most important and influential.

Case study: Boethius and eternity

The thought experiment at the opening of this chapter is based on a true story about the Roman philosopher Boethius (480–524 CE). He was at the top of his game, with a successful career in the Roman senate and a thriving family, when the Germanic king he had been advising suddenly turned against him. After an excruciating year of waiting in prison, he was cruelly executed. While in prison, he wrote a book called *The Consolation of Philosophy*, in which he and 'Lady Philosophy' explore various philosophical puzzles concerning fate.

In his solution to the problem of how God can know the future without eliminating free will, Boethius develops a new concept of eternity. Prior to Boethius, many philosophers took 'eternity' to mean time without beginning or end. Boethius contends, however, that when we call God 'eternal' we don't just mean that he lacks beginning and end, but that his entire infinite life occurs simultaneously – that is, without any distinction between past, present or future. He writes:

> God is eternal; in this judgement all rational beings agree. Let us, then, consider what eternity is. For this word carries with it a revelation alike of the Divine nature and of the Divine knowledge. Now, eternity is the possession of endless life whole and perfect at a single moment. [...] For it is one thing for existence to be endlessly prolonged, which was what Plato ascribed to the world, another for the whole of an endless life to be embraced in the present, which is manifestly a property peculiar to the Divine mind. [...] So, if we are minded to give things their right names, we shall follow Plato in saying that God indeed is eternal, but the world everlasting.

> Boethius, *The Consolation of Philosophy*, Book V, Ch. 6 (http://www.gutenberg.org/files/14328/14328-h/14328-h.htm)

According to Boethius, to be everlasting is to endure in a succession of moments without beginning or end, while to be eternal is to endure in a single moment without beginning or end. (It should further be noted that, when Boethius speaks of 'the world' being everlasting, he is referring to the universe as a whole, not just to the planet Earth.)

Since Boethius was a Christian, he presumably accepted the biblical story according to which God created the universe out of nothing. And yet, here we see him endorsing Plato's view – also held by Aristotle and many other pre-Christian thinkers – that the universe has always existed.

The question of whether and how the universe could be everlasting soon became a hotly debated topic.

Cosmological proof

Aquinas's First Way is also known as the **cosmological proof**. Although there are actually a number of different types of cosmological proofs, each rests on empirical observations concerning the universe's basic operating principles.

Aquinas begins by pointing out that it is evident to our senses that some things in the world are in motion. He then raises the question, how did this motion come to be?

Suppose you see a stone moving across a level floor. It would naturally occur to you to ask: what's moving that stone? Suppose you look closer and realize that a long stick or staff is pushing the stone. Now you have an answer to your question. But it would be strange for you to be satisfied with this answer because it prompts a new question – what's moving the staff? Suppose you look closer and realize that a man's hand is pushing the staff. Now you have an answer to your second question. Would it be strange to be satisfied at last?

Not necessarily. You now know how the stone is moving across the floor: someone is pushing a staff, which is pushing the stone. You don't need to ask further what's moving the man because he is capable of moving himself.

At a deeper level, however, you do have to ask what's moving the man. In order for him to push the staff, neurons must fire in his brain, blood must flow through his body, muscles must contract, and so on. All of this has been going on in his body for a long time, and he didn't start any of it. What moved the man?

We might trace the man's vital functions back to his first moment of existence and credit his parents with setting him in motion. But then we would immediately have to ask the same question about them, and so on, and so on. We won't be satisfied until we come at last to the beginning of the chain – something whose motion doesn't need to be explained because it isn't moving – an unmoved mover. Aquinas asks, what could this be other than God?

The Big Bang

The first question that arises for the cosmological proof is: why should the unmoved mover we are seeking be identified with God? Astrophysics today provides plenty of empirical evidence about the origins of the universe. Because we can observe the universe expanding, we know that it came from a cosmic explosion – 'The Big Bang'.

Going back to our example, we can trace the stone to the staff, the staff to the man, the man to his parents, his parents to their parents, and so on back through the primordial soup, ultimately to the Big Bang. The Big Bang is the unmoved mover at which the explanation stops.

> *Therefore, whatever is in motion must be put in motion by another. If that by which it is put in motion be itself put in motion, then this also must needs be put in motion by another, and that by another again. But this cannot go on to infinity, because then there would be no first mover, and, consequently, no other mover; seeing that subsequent movers move only inasmuch as they are put in motion by the first mover; as the staff moves only because it is put in motion by the hand. Therefore it is necessary to arrive at a first mover, put in motion by no other; and this everyone understands to be God.*
> Thomas Aquinas, *Summa Theologica* Pt. I, Art. 2 Qu. 3 (http://www.newadvent.org/summa/1002htm#article2)

Granted, Aquinas could not have known about the Big Bang. If pressed on this point, however, he might argue that the Big Bang is not a satisfying explanation. We can further ask: where did the Big Bang come from? An atheist might insist that it randomly popped into existence out of nowhere. But this seems to be an evasion of the issue.

Theists, in contrast, have a much more satisfying answer. Of course, we can trace the causal chain all the way back to the Big Bang. But we can't stop there. The Big Bang itself must have been created by God.

The atheist might object that this only pushes the problem back a step because now God in turn needs to be explained.

But this misses the crucial point with which we began – that only things that are moving need to be explained. While the Big Bang was itself moving, God was not. Because God is a non-physical being, he can cause motion without himself having to move. God is therefore the best candidate for the unmoved mover.

The everlasting universe

Some atheists are content to see the Big Bang as a 'brute fact' – meaning the end of the explanation. For atheists who are not content with this answer, however, there is another option.

While contemporary astrophysics has successfully established the Big Bang, it has not established that the Big Bang was the beginning. At present, we have no way of knowing what may or may not have occurred before the Big Bang. The Big Bang could have been the result of a prior universe collapsing, the latest in an infinite chain of expanding and collapsing universes. This 'oscillating model' implies that the universe is everlasting.

It's difficult to conceive of a beginningless series of universes because everything we observe around us seems to have a beginning: the opening scene in a movie, breaking ground for a house, the birth of a baby and so on. But God himself is supposed to be beginningless – if it is possible to conceive of him as having existed for all eternity, then it is equally possible to conceive of matter as having done so. Plato and Aristotle were entirely convinced that matter is neither created nor destroyed, but rather cycles through infinite changes.

Elsewhere in his work, Aquinas himself admits that there is no way to rule out this possibility. Yet he thinks his cosmological proof should be persuasive. To those who are inclined to believe that the universe had no beginning, he would ask: why does this infinite cycle exist rather than nothing at all? He would argue that, even if the universe is everlasting, it cannot be a brute fact.

Does it make more sense to allow God to function as the brute fact at the bottom of the explanation? This is a deep question that everyone must answer for themselves. Meanwhile, Aquinas has another trick up his sleeve.

The teleological proof

In the Fifth Way, Aquinas turns from the origin of the entire universe to the organization of our little corner of it.

The Fifth Way is taken from the governance of the world. We see that things which lack intelligence, such as natural bodies, act for an end, and this is evident from their acting always, or nearly always, in the same way, so as to obtain the best result. Hence it is plain that not fortuitously, but designedly, do they achieve their end. Now whatever lacks intelligence cannot move towards an end, unless it be directed by some being endowed with knowledge and intelligence; as the arrow is shot to its mark by the archer. Therefore some intelligent being exists by whom all natural things are directed to their end; and this being we call God.

Thomas Aquinas, *Summa Theologica* Pt. I, Art. 2 Qu. 3 (http://www.newadvent.org/summa/1002htm#article2)

The Fifth Way is called the **teleological proof** from the Greek word for 'purpose'.

Have you ever observed the life of an ordinary squirrel? She gathers dry leaves and builds a nest high up in a tree to protect herself and her family from predators. She communicates with other squirrels through distinctive chirps. She collects acorns and buries them in the ground where she can find them again during the long, hard winter.

A squirrel is busy, busy, busy all day long. But does she ever stop and think, 'I'd better keep busy so I can live happily ever after.' No, she does not. Her brain is the size of a walnut. She doesn't really think anything. She is simply programmed to do what she does.

The same is true for the rest of nature. Rivers flow, trees reach for the sun and geese fly south, all without an ounce of intelligence. Not only do individual members of the natural world achieve extraordinary results without thought, they all work together to achieve an interdependent system that will positively awe anyone who takes the time to notice it.

This complex and stunningly beautiful system could not have come about by chance, Aquinas asserts. It must have been created by God.

Spotlight

Three engineering students were sitting around talking between classes, when one brought up the question of who designed the human body.

One of the students insisted that it must have been an electrical engineer because of the perfection of the nerves and synapses.

Another argued that it had to have been a mechanical engineer because the system of levers and pulleys is ingenious.

'You're both wrong,' the third student said. 'The human body was designed by an architect. Who else would have put a toxic waste pipe through a recreation area?'

Evolution

Aquinas's argument hinges on the claim that God is the only plausible explanation for the design we observe in the natural world. There is another explanation, however – one that Aquinas was dimly aware of.

Aristotle reports an idea proposed by one of his predecessors, Empedocles, that has come to be known as the **theory of evolution through natural selection**. Why do animals have sharp teeth in front and flat teeth at the back, Empedocles asks. His answer? Because this works best for survival. Those whose teeth didn't happen to grow this way died out. Empedocles talks about unsuccessful species that have disappeared, leaving the successes that we see around us.

It wasn't until the nineteenth century, however, that compelling evidence for this theory came to light. The English naturalist Charles Darwin (1809–82) showed that the wonder of the natural world is exactly what we should expect to see, given the four basic principles by which it operates:

1 **Replication:** Organisms reproduce themselves, passing their characteristics on to their offspring.

2 **Random mutation:** Replication is never perfect. Each generation brings new characteristics, some better and some worse for survival.

3 **Harsh conditions:** In the fight for survival, those with even a slight advantage will be more likely to reproduce, causing small changes in the species.

4 **Aeons of time:** Small changes in the species add up from generation to generation, resulting in new species.

This process, evolution through natural selection, creates the appearance of intelligence in the natural world. It looks as though someone must have programmed the squirrel to take care of her family. But replication, random mutation, harsh conditions and aeons of time can programme a species just as easily as an intelligent designer can.

Given that there is now so much scientific support for evolution, fewer and fewer people reject it the way Aquinas did. It's more common now to combine the theory with theism, insisting that God works through the fourfold process described above.

Note, however, that, in order to function as an argument for the existence of God, the teleological proof needs to show that there is some crucial role for God to play – something evolution cannot explain about the natural world. Otherwise, evolution alone is enough – there is no justification for the inference that God must exist.

Anthropic considerations

In the search for something only God could have accomplished, some theists raise the question, why is the universe just right for life? If just one of the constants that govern nature, such as the strength of gravity, were different, then human beings could never have evolved. It seems extraordinary that so many coincidences (known as **anthropic coincidences**, from the Greek word for 'man') combined to make a warm, hospitable planet possible within the vast, cold expanse of outer space. Isn't it more likely that someone deliberately arranged things?

The problem with this line of reasoning is that it cuts the other way as well. It may at first seem amazing that the strength of gravity is exactly right for you to be here, reading this book right now. But, on second thoughts, given that you are here, reading this book right now, it would be amazing if the strength of gravity weren't exactly right. That is, if the earth weren't hospitable, then we wouldn't be here to wonder about it. This insight has been developed into the **anthropic principle**, according to which observations of the universe have to be compatible with the observer.

Considering that the universe is so big (perhaps infinitely big) and so old (perhaps infinitely old), it seems highly likely – even necessary – that the conditions for a hospitable planet would come together somewhere, sometime. It's a bit like the lottery. Don't buy a ticket, because it's extremely unlikely that you'll win. But someone or other has to win.

Perhaps a more promising line of defence against Darwin's challenge concerns essentially anthropic qualities, such as 'true love'. If there is no God, and everything is the result of natural necessity, then human attachments can be explained purely scientifically. Are you willing to accept that the strong feelings you have for your lover are nothing but hormones geared for reproduction? Needless to say, arguments can be developed on both sides and the jury is still out.

Key ideas

A priori: Knowledge that is prior to, or independent of, experience

A posteriori: Knowledge that is after, or dependent upon, experience

Anthropic coincidence: The universe's fundamental constants happen to fall within the narrow range compatible with human life

Anthropic principle: Observations of the universe have to be compatible with the observer

Big Bang: The cosmic explosion that started the universe

Brute fact: The event at the end of the explanation

Cosmological proof: Aquinas's argument for the existence of God based on empirical considerations about the universe's basic operative principles

Eternal: Enduring in a single moment without beginning or end

Everlasting: Enduring in a succession of moments without beginning or end

Evolution through natural selection: The 'design' in nature is produced by the four principles of replication, random mutation, harsh conditions and aeons of time

Oscillating model: The theory according to which the Big Bang is the result of a prior universe collapsing, the latest in an infinite chain of expanding and collapsing universes

Teleological proof: Aquinas's argument for the existence of God based on design observed in nature

Fact-check

1 What does it mean to be eternal, according to Boethius?
   a To endure in a succession of moments without beginning or end
   b To endure in a single moment without beginning or end
   c To exist timelessly without changing
   d To exist in time without changing

2 Which of the following is not one of the four principles by which evolution operates?
   a Rapid speed
   b Replication
   c Random mutation
   d Harsh conditions

3 Aquinas's First Way conceives of God as which of the following?
   a A man on a mountaintop viewing a caravan on the road below
   b Supreme being
   c Everlasting rather than eternal
   d The unmoved mover

4 According to the oscillating model...
   a The universe has no beginning
   b The universe has to have just the right conditions for life
   c God is eternal rather than everlasting
   d Species have to adapt to harsh conditions in order to survive

5 Which of the following asserts that observations have to be compatible with the observer?
   a Evolution by natural selection
   b The anthropic principle
   c The cosmological proof
   d The teleological proof

6 Which of the following found evidence for the theory that challenges the teleological proof of God's existence?
   a Empedocles
   b Anselm
   c Thomas Aquinas
   d Charles Darwin

7 Which of the following would challenge the theory of evolution by natural selection?
- **a** Dinosaur bones
- **b** Free will
- **c** HIV/AIDS
- **d** Nuclear war

8 Aquinas argues that natural bodies, like squirrels…
- **a** Are intelligent
- **b** Act for an end
- **c** Exist in reality
- **d** Are a priori

9 Aquinas's Five Ways are…
- **a** Innatist
- **b** Idealist
- **c** A priori
- **d** A posteriori

10 A brute fact is…
- **a** An indisputable point
- **b** An explanation of evil
- **c** The end of the explanation
- **d** A fact about violent animals

Dig deeper

Ralph McInerny, *Aquinas* (Polity Press, 2004).

Eleonore Stump, *Aquinas* (Routledge, 2003).

John Wippel, *The Metaphysical Thought of Thomas Aquinas: From Finite Being to Uncreated Being* (Catholic University of America Press, 2000).

5

Descartes and the soul

'Doubt is the origin of wisdom.'
René Descartes

In this chapter you will learn:

▶ *about Descartes's method of doubt and its connection to rationalism*

▶ *why there is just one thing of which you can be absolutely certain*

▶ *how Descartes attempts to escape solipsism*

▶ *the meaning of dualism*

▶ *about the mind-body problem*

▶ *the challenge qualia present*

▶ *the meaning of folk psychology and why materialists reject it.*

Thought experiment: the matrix

You open your Internet browser and a man's face appears on your screen. He addresses you by name.

'These pop-up ads are getting out of control,' you mumble to yourself as you attempt to click to a different screen. The face does not budge. He calls your name again. You hit the power button on your computer in frustration. It does not turn off.

'I have some very important information for you,' the man says. His eyes follow yours when you move. He can see you.

'What the hell is going on?' you exclaim.

'There's no reason to be alarmed,' he reassures you with a small smile. 'It's good news, actually. I'm here to tell you that you've been selected for a unique experiment.'

'Not interested,' you snap.

'On the contrary – you've already volunteered,' he responds. 'You just don't remember.'

The man goes on to tell you that, when you volunteered for the experiment, you were given drugs that put you in a deep and long-term sleep. You were then attached to electrodes that connected your brain to a sophisticated virtual-reality program.

You sit dumbfounded.

'Look around you,' says the man. 'Nothing you seem to see is real.'

You look around you, trying to picture everything you see as virtual reality. You examine your hand and rub your fingers together.

'We are able to simulate all five senses,' the man adds. 'Nothing you touch is real. Nothing you smell, or taste, or hear is real.'

You sit silently for a moment, weighing the possibility he presents. 'Why don't I remember agreeing to this?' you ask.

'All your memories have been replaced,' he replies. 'Think of what you did yesterday, or what you were like as a child.' He gives you a moment to think of these things before continuing. 'All of those thoughts have been supplied by our program.'

A shiver runs down your spine. 'My family...'

'...doesn't exist. That is, you may or may not have a family, but, if you do, it certainly wouldn't be the one you seem to remember. All of your memories about where you come from are part of the program, as is your physical appearance.'

You look down at your body – it seems so familiar. The old shoes on your feet, the mole on your arm... You put your hand to your head, feel your face and run your fingers through your hair.

'You don't really look like that...' he says. 'You're actually not even human. We made up the human race, and the entire planet Earth.'

You take a deep breath. 'If I'm not human, then what am I?'

'I can't tell you.'

You narrow your eyes at him. He shrugs. 'You don't believe me? True, I might be lying, but I might not... How can you be sure?'

'What is the purpose of all of this?'

'To remove all certainties.'

You stop and think. Is there anything you can be certain of in these circumstances? Has the experiment been successful?

Think again

The French philosopher René Descartes (1596–1650) is considered the first modern philosopher. The period known as 'modern philosophy' runs from around the end of the Renaissance to the beginning of the twentieth century, when 'post-modernism' begins.

Modern philosophy is marked by a new focus on epistemology. As we have seen, Plato and Anselm take an 'innatist' approach, which begins with the assumption that there are truths to be discovered deep within our minds. Meanwhile, Aristotle and Aquinas take an empiricist approach, looking for truths in the external world. Each philosopher is committed to his approach without doing much to defend it. Modern philosophers finally undertook this defence.

Though motivated neither by Plato's ideal world of Forms nor by Anselm's faith, Descartes champions their side of the debate. The fundamental theme in Descartes's philosophy is reason: we discover innate truths through the power of clear thinking. In his hands, the inward-looking approach we have seen running through Plato and Anselm becomes the epistemology known as **rationalism**.

The method of doubt

Descartes was already a celebrated mathematician and scientist when he published his most famous idea. The same idea, also featured in the thought experiment at the beginning of this chapter, became the basis of the 1999 science fiction movie *The Matrix*. The idea is simply this: what if we are living in a virtual reality?

Bear in mind that Descartes had this brainchild back in the seventeenth century, long before computers were invented. He dreamed it up in a work called *Meditations on First Philosophy*, in which he set out to explain to his fans the secret of his intellectual success. (Ever done any analytic geometry? Well, Descartes invented – yes, invented – that. It was just one of his many ground-breaking intellectual contributions.)

The secret of Descartes's success was doubt – the method of doubt. Descartes argues that, if you want to discover true knowledge, your first step must be to question absolutely everything that you have ever believed.

This may seem a strange way to begin. Wouldn't it make more sense to build on whatever knowledge you already have?

It would, if your alleged 'knowledge' could be trusted. If, however, you are like most people (just about everyone, actually), the beliefs you call 'knowledge' have been far too carelessly acquired – picked up along the way in life without sufficient scrutiny. You believe whatever you think you see and hear. Even worse, you believe what others tell you they saw and heard. The problem – which you will be reluctant to face! – is that your mind is riddled with falsehoods that must be rooted out.

It's difficult to root out falsehoods in your own mind. They feel so comfortable and familiar – just as comfortable and familiar as the truth. In fact, it's almost impossible to distinguish between the two. The only solution is to clear-cut the forest – rid the mind of all beliefs, whether true or false – and begin again, this time carefully allowing only true beliefs to take root. But how?

The malignant demon

> I will suppose, then, [...] that some malignant demon, who is at once exceedingly potent and deceitful, has employed all his artifice to deceive me; I will suppose that the sky, the air, the earth, colours, figures, sounds, and all external things, are nothing better than the illusions of dreams, by means of which this being has laid snares for my credulity; I will consider myself as without hands, eyes, flesh, blood, or any of the senses, and as falsely believing that I am possessed of these; I will continue resolutely fixed in this belief, and if indeed by this means it be not in my power to arrive at the knowledge of truth, I shall at least do what is in my power, viz. [suspend my judgement], and guard with settled purpose against giving my assent to what is false, and being imposed upon by this deceiver, whatever be his power and artifice.
>
> Descartes, Meditation I, *Meditations on First Philosophy* (http://oregonstate.edu/instruct/phl302/texts/descartes/meditations/Meditation1html)

Setting an example for his readers, Descartes undertakes to convince himself to let go of all of his dearly held assumptions. His line of reasoning goes like this:

▷ My senses have often deceived me. For example, when I insert a stick in water, it looks bent even though it's really straight. Why should I trust my eyes when they have lied to me so many times?

▷ Moreover, I have experienced vivid dreams. While reading this book I might fall asleep and dream that I am reading this book. So how do I know whether or not I'm dreaming right now?

▶ Worse yet, I've heard of people who have been hospitalized for mental illness. They are completely convinced that they are kings and queens ... or ordinary people trying to teach themselves philosophy. How, therefore, do I know that I'm not in a hospital suffering from such a delusion?

Just in case these possibilities aren't worrisome enough, Descartes finally proposes the worst-case scenario, as described in the extract above. Descartes does not need computer technology to invent the ultimate test for the mind. His malignant demon (sometimes called the 'evil genius') does the trick. Will any of our beliefs survive?

The cogito

When we take Descartes's thought experiment seriously we find ourselves in a strange, disembodied state, popularly known as the 'brain in a vat'. You are nothing but an intellect floating in nothingness, completely severed from everything you thought you knew and loved.

Is there anything you can truly claim to know under these circumstances? You know nothing about your body, your history or your world. It seems as though you can't be certain of anything at all.

Descartes discovered, however, that there is one thing of which you can be certain, even as a brain in a vat. He discovered it by thinking about thinking.

In order to think – even if all your thoughts are all falsehoods – you have to exist. Therefore you can be absolutely certain of your own existence.

This discovery is called **the cogito**, short for the Latin phrase *cogito ergo sum*, which means 'I think therefore I am'. It is still today regarded as one of the most indisputable proofs ever invented. But is it enough?

> *Thinking is another attribute of the soul; and here I discover what properly belongs to myself. This alone is inseparable from me. I am – I exist: this is certain; but how often? As often as I think; for perhaps it would even happen, if I should wholly cease to think, that I should at the same time altogether cease to be. I now admit nothing that is not necessarily true. I am therefore, precisely speaking, only a thinking thing, that is, a mind (mens sive animus), understanding, or reason, terms whose signification was before unknown to me. I am, however, a real thing, and really existent; but what thing? The answer was, a thinking thing.*
>
> Descartes, Meditation II, *Meditations on First Philosophy* (http://oregonstate.edu/instruct/phl302/texts/descartes/meditations/Meditation2html)

Spotlight

Descartes walks into a bar. The bartender walks up to him and says, 'Would you care for a drink?' Descartes replies, 'I think not,' and disappears.

God and the world

If we were to stop with the cogito we would be condemned to **solipsism** – the view that only the self exists. Take a moment right now to try this view out.

Feeling a little lonely? So did Descartes. He resolved to build on his gains, continuing in the following way:

1 So, I know for certain that I am a thinking thing. What shall I think about? The best thing I can think of is God.

2 God is a being far superior to me. In fact, he is infinite. How did I think of him? If I am the only being in existence, then I must have made up the idea of God all by myself. But I am finite. Surely, it's impossible for a finite being to think of an infinite being. Therefore I am not alone after all – another being, an infinite being, must exist.

3 Perhaps the malignant demon gave me the idea of God. But God is infinitely good and not at all malignant. A malignant demon – whether he is finite or infinite – could not have conceived of infinite goodness.

4 One might suppose that I or the malignant demon could conceive of God by negation. If I'm hungry, then I can think of being full, and, if I'm tired, then I can think of being awake. Therefore if I think of my limitations, then I can think of limitlessness.

5 But the idea I generate by negating my own limitations is not the same as the idea I have of God. The idea I have of God is such a clear and distinct idea of infinite perfection that it could not have come from anything but a being that is infinitely perfect.

6 Therefore, an infinitely perfect being must exist.

7 Could this infinitely perfect being be my malignant demon? That is, could God himself be systematically deceiving me about the world?

8 Surely not, because an infinitely perfect being is all good. Granted, an all-good being could allow careless thinkers to be deceived by their own carelessness. But he could never allow someone who is trying to be a careful thinker to be continuously and completely deceived. Much less could he deliberately cause such deception.

9 Therefore the world must exist.

Hey presto! – starting with just his own existence, Descartes quickly restores the reality he believed in before beginning his meditation. He has learned that, if he thinks carelessly, he may come to false conclusions about the world. But if he uses reason, striving always for the standard of 'clear and distinct' ideas, he should be able to attain new knowledge.

Granting that Descartes's method of doubt succeeds in proving the existence of the self, is it equally successful in proving the existence of God and the world?

The Cartesian circle

Descartes's proof of God and the world relies crucially on the notion of the 'clear and distinct idea'. His reasoning can be summarized as follows:

1 I have a clear and distinct idea of God.

2 My idea of God is so clear and distinct that it must have come from God.

3 Therefore God must exist.

This way of interpreting Descartes's argument shows that it suffers from the same problem as Anselm's ontological proof, which we saw in the last chapter: it appears to be circular because it assumes the very thing it's trying to prove.

Descartes makes a distinction between two different kinds of ideas – those that are clear and distinct versus those that are vague and hazy. He further claims that the clear and distinct ideas are guaranteed to be true. What could possibly secure this guarantee other than God? Conversely, if God doesn't exist, there's no guarantee that clear and distinct ideas are true.

What's to stop our malignant demon from transmitting two different types of falsehood to us – those that seem clear and distinct as well as those that seem vague and hazy? Presumably, being so powerful, he could do this just as easily as you are able to speak loudly or mumble softly. Evidently, Descartes's proof is not immune to his own method of doubt.

Although Descartes and his followers can develop a response to this criticism, it will be a challenge for them to reach their goal of restoring reality.

Dualism

Descartes's proof of God and the world was never as enthusiastically received as the cogito itself. In facing down the malignant demon, Descartes shows that, while we can doubt the existence of our bodies, we cannot doubt the existence of our minds. This seems to support the metaphysical view known as

dualism, according to which human beings are composed of two different kinds of substance: physical and mental.

The physical aspect of the human being includes everything that can be empirically observed, and so, of course, it includes the brain. The mental aspect includes the thoughts and feelings that can be observed only introspectively, where introspection is understood as a self-reflexive examination of one's own consciousness.

Dualists believe the brain alone is insufficient to explain all our thoughts and feelings. In their view, our consciousness, while connected to the brain, goes beyond its capacity. Dualists sometimes call this mental aspect 'mind' and sometimes 'soul', treating the two terms as synonymous.

Of course, the idea that each human being possesses a soul has a long history in many religions. Descartes himself was at least nominally a member of the Catholic Church, which holds that the soul survives the death of the body. Anyone who wants eternal life will have to believe in a non-physical aspect of themselves.

But wanting eternal life is not a good reason for believing in the existence of the soul. After all, no matter how badly children want presents to appear in the Christmas stockings they hang, they cannot thereby make Santa Claus real. The truth is that ordinary mums and dads are sufficient to explain all the gifts that have ever appeared in Christmas stockings.

Is the brain alone sufficient to explain all our thoughts and feelings? If so, there is no reason to believe in the soul.

Spotlight

According to Descartes's dualism, the body is a machine controlled by the soul. Since animals don't have souls in his view, they are pure machines, incapable of feeling pain. They cry out when you strike them, but only in the same way that a musical instrument sounds when struck. Descartes is said to have tested this theory by practising vivisection (live dissection) on cats – or perhaps he was just getting his revenge against cats because a cat had bitten off his little toe when he was a child.

Qualia

Dualists argue that there is something very significant that the brain alone is insufficient to account for – namely, **qualia**.

Suppose I place you in a futuristic CAT scan and ask you to think of your lover. I can observe the neurons firing in your brain. I can measure how your brain chemistry changes. Perhaps I can even simulate the same changes in my own brain. Nevertheless, I cannot observe your love. No matter how sophisticated my instruments are, I will never know what your love feels like introspectively.

This subjective conscious experience – what your love feels like – is a quale. Our minds are full of qualia, from something as simple as how cinnamon smells to something as complex as what it's like to perform a triple axel. A complete scientific description of these phenomena from the outside does not capture what they are from the inside. Hence, it seems that our minds must be something more than just brains.

Nevertheless, there is a real mystery concerning how mental substance could be connected to physical substance. Descartes's critics say that his view makes human beings look like 'a ghost in a machine' because the soul is supposed to control the body the way a person drives a car. But how can a ghost push or pull the buttons and levers to make a machine move? Without any physical substance, its hands would go right through the controls!

Likewise, how does the soul move the body? We know how neurons stimulate muscles to contract and propel our bodies through space. But how would something non-physical in turn stimulate a neuron? Dualists want to say that your love can make you do something – such as bake a birthday cake. How will your soul cause your body to take action? This is known as the **mind–body problem**.

In Descartes's day, the function of the pineal gland was unknown. Descartes therefore hypothesized that it could be the seat of some kind of transference between mental and physical substance. Now that we know the function of the pineal gland, however, this hypothesis is no longer taken seriously.

Case study: materialism

Materialism, the view that human beings are purely physical bodies, has grown increasingly popular since Descartes's day. One of its most vocal exponents is the American philosopher Paul Churchland (1942–), who maintains that qualia do not exist.

According to Churchland, the mistaken belief in qualia is a product of common language. Because people regularly talk about how they feel 'on the inside', it seems that these feelings have objective existence.

By analogy, consider a society of people who believe in witches. They talk about witches all the time and think they observe witchery playing an active role in the world. It would be hard to convince these people that their witch concept is nothing but 'folk psychology' – a primitive and inaccurate explanation. Churchland writes:

> *Modern theories of mental dysfunction led to the elimination of witches from our serious ontology. The concepts of folk psychology – belief, desire, fear, sensation, pain, joy, and so on – await a similar fate, according to the view at issue. And when neuroscience has matured to the point where the poverty of our current conceptions is apparent to everyone, and the superiority of the new framework is established, we shall then be able to set about reconceiving our internal states and activities, within a truly adequate conceptual framework at last. Our explanations of one another's behaviour will appeal to such things as our neuropharmacological states, the neural activity in specialized anatomical areas, and whatever other states are deemed relevant by the new theory.*
> Paul Churchland, *Matter and Consciousness* (MIT Press, 1999), pp. 44–5

Notice that Churchland's list of folk psychology concepts does not include love. Will neuroscience one day make it possible for us to eliminate all talk of love? Would this be a good thing, or would it be good to continue to speak of love even if it doesn't really exist?

Dualists continue to look for the connection between mind and body elsewhere, such as in the mysterious properties of quantum mechanics. As science progresses, many of these hypotheses, like the pineal gland hypothesis, will be ruled out – but perhaps not all. It remains to be seen whether science will ever be able to provide a fully adequate account of our thoughts and feelings.

Key ideas

The cogito: Descartes's proof of his own existence

Dualism: The view that human beings are composed of two substances: body and soul

Folk psychology: A primitive and inaccurate explanation

Introspection: A self-reflexive examination of one's own consciousness

Materialism: The view that human beings are purely physical bodies and that there is no such thing as the soul

Mind–body problem: The mystery concerning how the mental substance could be connected to physical substance

Qualia: Instances of subjective, conscious experience

Rationalism: The view that we discover innate truths through the power of clear thinking

Solipsism: The view that only the self exists

Fact-check

1 Descartes's rationalism developed from which of the following?
   a Materialism
   b Innatism
   c Empiricism
   d Solipsism

2 What is the purpose of Descartes's malignant demon?
   a To question eternal life
   b To see whether anything is certain
   c To prove that the soul is folk psychology
   d To promote meditation

3 Which of the following is a problem with Descartes's argument for the existence of God?
   a It seems circular
   b It seems vague
   c It seems hazy
   d It seems malignant

4 Descartes concludes that God must exist because he is which of the following?
   a Loving
   b Limitless
   c Infinite
   d Eternal

5 Which of the following best represents the soul and the body according to Descartes?
   a God and a demon
   b A caterpillar and its cocoon
   c Two lovers
   d A captain and his ship

6 Which of the following is an example of folk psychology?
   a Neurons
   b Demons
   c Qualia
   d Dreams

7 Which of the following best demonstrates the mind–body problem?
- **a** A demon playing tricks
- **b** A witch casting spells
- **c** A ghost walking through walls
- **d** A cat howling in pain

8 Which of the following would deny that human beings have life after death?
- **a** Churchland
- **b** Descartes
- **c** Plato
- **d** Anselm

9 Someone who believes in only their own existence is which of the following?
- **a** A materialist
- **b** A rationalist
- **c** A solipsist
- **d** An innatist

10 What is the first thing Descartes is able to prove against the malignant demon?
- **a** That he exists
- **b** That God exists
- **c** That the world exists
- **d** That the malignant demon exists

Dig deeper

Steven M. Duncan, *The Proof of the External World: Cartesian Theism and the Possibility of Knowledge* (James Clarke & Co., 2008)

Tom Sorell, *Descartes: A Very Short Introduction* (Oxford, 2001)

Bernard Williams, *Descartes: The Project of Pure Enquiry* (Routledge, 2005)

6

Hobbes and freedom

'The condition of man: war of everyone against everyone.'
Thomas Hobbes

In this chapter you will learn:

▶ *the meaning of free will*
▶ *why determinists reject free will*
▶ *how Hobbes explains human choices*
▶ *how compatibilism attempts to save a measure of human freedom*
▶ *the meaning of the state of nature*
▶ *why Hobbes thinks we need an absolute sovereign*
▶ *why Rousseau favours a republic over an absolute sovereign*
▶ *about social contract theory and how the veil of ignorance supports it.*

Thought experiment: change your life?

You are window shopping in China Town. The evening air is cool and breezy. The pavement is strewn with festive lights. From each door you pass wafts a new flavour, from musky incense, to fresh fish, to sweet-and-sour chicken.

Ahead you see a shrunken, wrinkled Chinese woman with a basket. As you approach, she holds up a fortune cookie and smiles toothlessly at you.

'You buy?' she asks.

You hesitate and pat your pocket absently for spare change. You actually wouldn't mind buying a fortune cookie. On the other hand, you don't feel like stopping to dig your wallet out of your backpack.

You smile and shake your head. 'No thank you.'

The woman's eyes grow wide and she stops smiling. 'Could change your life!'

You sigh and begin reaching for your backpack.

As you shrug its strap off your shoulders, you catch the scent of fresh pastries. It seems to be coming from a bakery across the street.

You turn away from the woman, shaking your head firmly this time.

She puts her hand out to keep you from leaving, but you angle around her, stepping off the narrow pavement into the street.

A deafening screech of tyres whips your head around just in time to feel the cold, hard front of a bus slam into your face.

For an instant, you feel excruciating pain.

Then nothing.

You are looking at the Chinese woman again – just her face, surrounded by darkness. Without speaking, she somehow communicates the following message to you.

'You are in limbo. Having been hit by a bus, you are on your way to the world of the dead. It's not too late, however, to turn back the clock and change your life. If you go back to the moment at which you were trying to decide whether or not to buy a fortune cookie and make the opposite choice this time, you will live instead of die.'

Of course, you are very happy to learn this and anxious to make the opposite choice.

The woman is ready to turn back the clock. She warns you, however, that everything has to be exactly the same the second time around. This means you won't have the knowledge of what will happen if you don't buy the fortune cookie.

'But if I don't know what's going to happen, I'll just do the same thing again!' you exclaim. 'I wanted to go to that bakery...'

'Are you a slave to your desires or are you free?' she interjects.

'What do you mean?'

'I mean, does desire determine what you do, or do you have free will?'

'Well... I have free will.'

'Then you don't have to do the same thing again. You were weighing two options. You were balanced equally between them. Your free will can break the tie – this time, the opposite way.'

Is she right? Can you make the opposite choice even if absolutely everything is exactly the same?

You've got to want it

The Catholic world view, which reigned supreme in Europe throughout the medieval period, asserts that human beings have free will. Free will is the ability to choose between two options in such a way that you are equally able to do either one.

Of course, even a mosquito seems to choose between options: it hovers by your arm... it dives in for the bite... then, at the last second, it veers away. But no one thinks mosquitoes have free will. Something – like a tiny breeze – must have caused it to veer away.

So, the phrase 'equally able to do either one' is a crucial part of the definition of free will. Free will is supposed to enable humans to 'veer away' without that 'tiny breeze'. That is, hovering over a piece of dark chocolate mousse truffle cake, you can dive in for the bite, or not, without anything but yourself to blame.

Free will is central to Catholicism because it holds that human beings are responsible for their sins. It wouldn't be just for God to punish us for our evil deeds if 'tiny breezes' are pushing us into them. If something about your situation causes you to steal, for example, then you can't be blamed for stealing.

Notice that, when it comes to ascribing responsibility for an evil deed, it doesn't matter whether the 'tiny breeze' is outside you or inside you. Suppose I force you to rob a bank by holding a gun to your back. Alternately, suppose I plant a microchip in your brain which programs you to rob the bank. Though the first cause is external and the second is internal, they amount to the same thing – you were not able to do otherwise, and so you are not responsible.

Free will requires the ability to do otherwise. Although this notion traces back to medieval Catholicism, it has become part of our culture. Everyone wants it and many claim to have it, whether or not they are Catholic.

Suppose you become a bank robber, and you try to excuse yourself by pointing out that your parents were bank robbers. Those who believe in free will (known as metaphysical libertarians) are going to say: 'Well, you can't blame your parents for how you turned out. Your circumstances do not force your decisions. With everything the same, you still could have made the opposite choice.'

A man can do what he wants, but not want what he wants.
Arthur Schopenhauer

Determinism

Although many people claim to believe in it, free will is actually a difficult notion to make sense of. The English philosopher Thomas Hobbes (1588–1679) was one of the first to point this out. Following his lead, many philosophers today reject free will in favour of some version of determinism. Determinism is the view that everything has a cause – even human choices, and so there is no such thing as free will.

For Hobbes, we are the slave to our desires. Suppose you decide to go for that piece of cake. This choice was caused by a desire within you, which was, in turn, caused by your memory of past experiences with cake. Your contrary desire to avoid unhealthy food was not as strong as your desire for cake, and so your desire for cake wins.

Determinists allow that everyone feels as though they have free will. This is because we have a lot of contrary desires within us. When our desires are battling against each other, we pause, hovering, feeling as though we could equally go either way. But, in fact, the strongest desire always wins.

Nor can we create new desires out of nothing. The desires we find within ourselves are caused by a multitude of factors – biology, environment, family, friends, media, etc., etc., many of which we are completely unaware of.

Sometimes, when we are trying to make a big decision, we need to 'sleep on it'. This allows all our subconscious desires to sift to the surface and break the apparent tie.

Metaphysical libertarians, in contrast, claim that we use free will to break the tie. In their view, this is the most important difference between human beings and animals. Some medieval philosophers went so far as to claim that a hungry donkey placed between two equally appealing piles of hay would starve to death for lack of free will to break the tie (a thought experiment that became known as 'Buridan's ass'). While animals are slaves to their desires, human beings are free.

Spotlight

Hobbes wanted to be a great mathematician like Descartes, but his efforts to square the circle were an abysmal failure. (Yes, he actually attempted to square the circle.) After a not-so-friendly meeting of the two men, Hobbes declared that Descartes's work outside mathematics was equally abysmal.

Human animals

Hobbes's entire philosophy can be understood as an effort to establish the similarity, rather than the difference, between human beings and animals.

Hobbes was the first modern thinker to defend a thoroughgoing materialism. Paving the way for contemporary materialists like Paul Churchland, whom we met in the previous chapter, Hobbes argues that everything existing in the universe is physical. (This left him with a very unconventional account of God, which is often interpreted as thinly veiled atheism.)

Even the mental lives of human beings can be understood in purely physical terms. In Hobbes's view, all of life is particles in motion. While plants are capable of only involuntary motion, animals move themselves through the world voluntarily. But what does 'voluntary' really mean?

Hobbes explains that, unlike plants, animals have sense organs connected to brains. When an external object (such as a cake) impacts our bodies (through smell or sight), it causes a tiny motion in our imagination, which in turn stimulates an 'effort', which may or may not have to compete with other efforts already in play.

Less intelligent animals, being unaware of the competition among their efforts, simply follow the strongest one. Because human beings are aware of the competition, in contrast, we are said to deliberate. Yet the strongest effort still wins, becoming a desire which sets our bodies in motion.

All human activity is driven by the desire for what we deem good – and aversion from what we deem bad.

Compatibilism

One might be inclined to suppose that determinism destroys human freedom. If freedom is an illusion, then we are left with fatalism, the view that it doesn't matter what we do because everything is fixed in advance. Although some philosophers, such as the ancient Stoics, were content to embrace fatalism, most regard it as a depressing and counterproductive outlook.

Hobbes, however, denies that determinism destroys human freedom. He argues that, although the causal process through which our choices are made is not compatible with free will, it is entirely compatible with 'liberty'. Liberty, as he defines it, is the absence of all the impediments to action that are not internal to the agent.

Hobbes presents an analogy to illustrate his view. Water is said to flow freely down the channel of a river when there is nothing, such as a dam, in its way. It is not free to move crosswise, because the banks are impediments. While we may say that the water wants to flow over the banks, we never say that it wants to flow up the channel. This is because it is in the nature of water to flow down and not up.

Likewise, if I tie you to a chair, we say that you are unfree because there is an external impediment preventing you from acting in accordance with your nature. Suppose, on the other hand, you are unable to get up from the chair because you are lame. We don't call you 'unfree' in that case, since the impediment is internal to you.

As a river flows freely the only way that it can, so, also, we choose freely in the only way that we can. There can be no such thing as free will because it would be a break in the causal chain. It would be an uncaused cause – impossible in a world driven by endless motion. We voluntarily carry out the necessary chain of causes that flows through us.

I conceive that nothing takes beginning from itself, but from the action of some other immediate agent without itself. And that, therefore, when first a man has an appetite or will to something, to which immediately before he had no appetite nor will, the cause of his will is not the will itself, but something else not in his own disposing. So that whereas it is out of controversy that of voluntary actions the will is the necessary cause, and by this which is said the will is also caused by other things whereof it disposes not, it follows that voluntary actions have all of them necessary causes and therefore are necessitated.

Thomas Hobbes, *Of Liberty and Necessity* (http://www.informationphilosopher. com/solutions/philosophers/hobbes/of_liberty_and_necessity.html)

This passage was a bold and deeply controversial statement of the view that has come to be known as **compatibilism**: human freedom is compatible with determinism because it does not consist in free will but rather in the absence of external constraints.

The state of nature

As we have seen in previous chapters, philosophers' metaphysical views strongly affect their approaches to ethics and political philosophy. This is clearly the case with Hobbes, whose contention that man is nothing more nor less than an animal brings him to a stark picture of human social relations.

In order to strip your mind of the biases and presuppositions that may cloud your understanding of human social relations, imagine what life would be like if there were no government. We often curse the government for subjecting us to so many rules and regulations while taxing our hard-earned income. But what would happen if government suddenly disappeared? Or, better yet, how might human beings have behaved before there was such a thing as government?

We would have behaved like animals.

> *In such condition there is no place for industry, because the fruit thereof is uncertain: and consequently no culture of the earth; no navigation, nor use of the commodities that may be imported by sea; no commodious building; no instruments of moving and removing such things as require much force; no knowledge of the face of the earth; no account of time; no arts; no letters; no society; and which is worst of all, continual fear, and danger of violent death; and the life of man, solitary, poor, nasty, brutish and short.*
> Thomas Hobbes, *Leviathan*, Ch. 13 (http://oregonstate.edu/instruct/phl302/texts/hobbes/leviathan-c.html)

Originating with Hobbes, this thought experiment, which has become known as **the state of nature,** has been extraordinarily influential throughout the history of political thought. (Bear in mind that, like all thought experiments, it is meant to be purely hypothetical. That is, whether there ever was or will be such a state of nature is irrelevant; the point is to explore the implications of the possibility.)

Hobbes asserts without qualification that the state of nature is a state of war pitting every man against every man. Although we may not always be actually fighting, we would be living without any security, among enemies. Hobbes argues that we must voluntarily accept and even welcome government, ugly as it may be, to lift us out of this intolerable condition and make a more noble life possible.

Spotlight

Born prematurely when his mother heard of the coming invasion of the Spanish Armada, Hobbes later said it was as though his mother gave birth to twins: 'myself and fear'. At least he was aware of his own obsession.

Absolute sovereign

In Hobbes's view, the only kind of government that can put an effective end to the war of all against all is an absolute sovereign. To underscore just how ugly and fearsome it needs to be, Hobbes called it the 'Leviathan' in reference to a giant, biblical sea monster. Although he is inclined to favour monarchy as the best form of absolute sovereignty, he is open to any form of government that has complete authority.

Complete authority is established through the powers of legislation, adjudication, enforcement, taxation, war-making and control of any official doctrine. (The last one is included in order to prevent such problems as the Inquisition, in which the Catholic Church expected governments to allow it to imprison and punish those who contradicted its teachings – a vivid concern for seventeenth-century intellectuals like Galileo, Descartes and Hobbes himself.) A government lacking or limited in any of its rightful powers creates competing allegiances, which readily become violent.

Case study: Rousseau and the 'noble savage'

Of course, there are those who disagree with Hobbes's claim that human life would be 'solitary, poor, nasty, brutish, and short' in the state of nature. The French philosopher Jean-Jacques Rousseau (1712–78) was content to grant that we would behave like animals, while rejecting Hobbes's characterization of them as depraved.

Rousseau was deeply interested in the native populations that European explorers were, in his day, discovering around the world. He developed a romantic picture of primitive culture – free as it is from the artificial complications of civilized life. In stark contrast to the frightening picture Hobbes presents, Rousseau writes:

> How few sufferings are felt by man living in a state of primitive simplicity! His life is almost entirely free from suffering and from passion; he neither fears nor feels death; if he feels it, his sufferings make him desire it; henceforth it is no evil in his eyes. If we were but content to be ourselves, we should have no cause to complain of our lot; but in the search for an imaginary good we find a thousand real ills. [...] Take away our fatal progress, take away our faults and our vices, take away man's handiwork, and all is well. Where all is well, there is no such thing as injustice.

> Jean-Jacques Rousseau, Emile (http://www.gutenberg.org/cache/epub/5427/pg5427html)

Rousseau insisted that human beings are born innocent and that it is unnatural societal expectations that corrupt us.

Rousseau does not naively propose that we attempt to emulate the 'noble savage'. In fact, it was his critics who invented that term. Rousseau admits that we human beings cannot squelch our ambitious imagination; it will always lure us out of a simple, animal existence. We therefore must secure civil society by establishing a government.

Rousseau agrees with Hobbes that we must voluntarily give up the freedom of the state of nature. His more optimistic assessment of human nature, however, leads him away from the idea of an absolute sovereign to a republic formed instead by the general will of the people.

Spotlight

It takes a fearsome creature to control the masses... and to entertain them, for 'Leviathan' is also the name of the newest roller-coaster in Canada's Wonderland. At 1,672 m (5,486 ft) long, 93 m (306 ft) tall and with a top speed of 148 km per hour (92 mph), it is one of the tallest and fastest in the world.

Although the sovereign must have complete authority in order to prevent war, the people retain certain rights against it, in Hobbes's view. Our obligation to obey extends exactly to the extent that the sovereign is able to protect us. This, after all, is why it exists.

Hobbes's critics contend that, by allowing individuals to retain rights against the sovereign, he contradicts his claim that the sovereign is absolute. For example, in Hobbes's state you would retain the right to self-defence and therefore the right to bear arms. But what if the sovereign passed a stringent gun-control law in the interest of public safety? If you felt it undermined your personal security, would you have the right to disobey? The devil is in details such as these – details that are often still highly controversial today.

The social contract

Hobbes was one of the first modern thinkers to propose that government is legitimate only when the people willingly agree to subject themselves to it. We make a covenant, or **social contract,** with one another to give up our natural rights in exchange for peace.

This social contract theory stands in stark contrast to **divine right theory,** according to which God gives royal families the right to rule over a region regardless of how the people who are living there happen to feel about it. It's easy to see why this mysterious, supernatural approach to government – which was the status quo throughout the medieval period and beyond – badly needed to be replaced. So the work of Hobbes, Rousseau and other social contract theorists was extremely important in the development of the modern state.

But social contract theory is not just a historical milestone. It continues to push political theorists into refining our conception of the state – its rights and limitations – and the nature of justice. After all, making a social contract isn't just a matter of agreeing to have a government; it requires deciding what that government should be like – what kinds of principles it should uphold and what services it should provide.

John Rawls (1921–2002) is a twentieth-century American philosopher who famously argued that we should make our social contract under a 'veil of ignorance'. The veil of ignorance is a thought experiment in which you imagine that you don't know anything about your personal identity – including your race, your gender, your religion, your sexual preference or whether you have a disability. This way, you won't inadvertently allow the social contract to be biased towards the advantage of any particular group. If you don't know whether or not you might be disabled, for example, you'll be sure to support laws that require public buildings to be accessible to disabled people. This veil of ignorance helps to guarantee a social contract that is as fair as possible to everyone – a philosophical interpretation of the old adage that 'justice is blind'.

Key ideas

Buridan's ass thought experiment: Would a hungry donkey placed between two equally appealing piles of hay starve to death for lack of free will to break the tie?

Compatibilism: The idea that human freedom is compatible with determinism because it does not consist in free will but rather in the absence of external constraints

Determinism: The view that everything has a cause – even human choices, and so there is no such thing as free will

Divine right theory: The theory that God gives royal families the right to rule over a region

Fatalism: The idea that it doesn't matter what we do because everything is fixed in advance

Free will: The ability to choose between two options in such a way that you are equally able to do either one

Metaphysical libertarians: Those who believe in free will

Social contract theory: Government is legitimate only when the people willingly agree to subject themselves to it

State of nature thought experiment: What would happen if there were no government?

Veil of ignorance thought experiment: What kind of a social contract would you make if you didn't know anything about your personal identity?

Fact-check

1 Which of the following causes our choices, according to Hobbes?
  a Free will
  b The strongest desire
  c God
  d Nothing

2 Metaphysical libertarians believe which of the following?
  a That human beings have the ability to do otherwise
  b That the sovereign should not be absolute
  c That everything has a cause
  d That we do not need to give up the freedom of the state of nature in exchange for peace

3 Which of the following is true, according to compatibilists?
  a Human beings sometimes have free will
  b Human beings never have free will
  c Human beings are innately innocent
  d Human beings are innately violent

4 Which of the following is a thought experiment that might lead to a justification of the state?
  a Fatalism
  b Change your life!
  c Buridan's ass
  d State of nature

5 How far does the people's obligation to obey the sovereign extend, according to Hobbes?
  a It extends as far as it is consistent with God's commands
  b It extends as far as the sovereign decides
  c It extends as far as the people decide
  d It extends as far as the sovereign is able to protect the people

6 Rousseau disagreed with Hobbes about which of the following claims?
  a Human beings are animals
  b Government ennobles human beings
  c Human beings are born innocent
  d Government is justified by social contract

7 For Hobbes, why are we human beings like rivers?
  a Because we can break the causal chain
  b Because we have to do what is in our nature
  c Because we move in unpredictable ways
  d Because we are all interconnected

8 Which of the following best describes all of life, according to Hobbes?
  a Mysterious
  b Motion
  c Divine
  d Free

9 Which of the following is Hobbes's motivation for making a social contract?
  a Innocence
  b Freedom
  c Fear
  d Desire

10 Free will requires which of the following?
  a The ability to do otherwise
  b The ability to disobey the sovereign
  c The ability to overcome external impediments
  d The ability to obey God

Dig deeper

Noel Malcolm, *Aspects of Hobbes* (Oxford University Press, 2002)

A.P. Martinich, *Hobbes* (Routledge, 2005)

Daniel C. Dennett, *Elbow Room: The Varieties of Free Will Worth Wanting* (MIT Press, 1984)

7

Locke and knowledge

'The mind is born a blank slate.'
John Locke

In this chapter you will learn:

▶ *about the problem of personal identity*

▶ *why Locke thinks memory makes us who we are*

▶ *the role of consciousness in personal responsibility*

▶ *the roots of political liberalism and its connection to empiricism*

▶ *why Locke introduces a distinction between objective and subjective qualities*

▶ *how pure empiricism can lead to idealism*

▶ *why Berkeley believes the world does not exist.*

Thought experiment: Thesean Shipese

The bad news is that you have contracted a very serious disease. The good news is that, while there is no cure, it is treatable.

The disease is called 'Thesean Shipese'. You were diagnosed last year when you went to hospital, complaining of excruciating pain in your left little toe. A host of doctors examined you and initiated your course of treatment.

First, your left little toe was removed.

Fortunately, extraordinary advancements in prosthetics made it possible to install an artificial toe that works just as well as the old one. Once the scar healed, it was virtually impossible to discern the replacement.

Unfortunately, this was just the beginning. Amputation of your left little toe did not stop the spread of the disease. By the time your scar healed, you had excruciating pain in the toe right next to your left little toe. And so it was removed and replaced by a new prosthetic toe.

But by the time this scar healed, the same followed for the next toe, and so on down the line. Once all your left toes were replaced one by one in succession, the disease moved into your foot.

What could you do? You had no choice but to let the doctors remove and replace your entire foot. This time they were hopeful that they had caught it before it moved into your leg.

But they were wrong.

As soon as the scar on your foot healed, you had excruciating pain in your left calf. The doctors decided to be more aggressive this time: they removed and replaced your entire left leg.

After the scar healed and you were just getting back to your regular life, your right little toe started acting up. This time, you didn't mess around. You asked the doctors to remove and replace your entire right leg. But then the disease moved first to your left arm and then to your right.

It has now been a year since you first contracted Thesean Shipese. All four of your prosthetic limbs are working just like your old ones did and you are ready to put the entire ordeal behind you.

But just this morning you began to feel that same excruciating pain again – this time, in your belly. In desperation, you hurry back to the hospital.

The doctors examine you and announce that you have the strongest strain of Thesean Shipese. The only course of treatment is to remove and replace your entire torso. Hopefully, the disease will not be able to spread above your neck.

If the disease does spread above your neck, however, the doctors are fully prepared to replace your head. They can transfer all the data from your brain into a prosthetic brain. They can also mould a replica of your face and match your hair (or give you a new look, if you like!). Once the scars heal, you should be able to return to your life with a completely new body, free from Thesean Shipese once and for all.

Are you willing to proceed with the treatment? Without it, the pain in your belly will grow and you will be dead within a week. On the other hand, what if your head has to be replaced? Would you be the same person? It seems new arms and legs don't affect your identity at all, and plenty of people have carried on with new organs. But with a new brain, who would you be after the surgery? Would you be the same person you were before the procedure or would you be someone new?

Shipshape

The foregoing scenario is based on an ancient thought experiment called the **Ship of Theseus**. Theseus was the legendary king of Athens, whose ship was reportedly preserved for many generations by replacing each one of its planks one by one, year by year.

The Ship of Theseus raises an important question about the identity of objects. When one of the planks on the ship is replaced, it's still essentially the same ship. But is it still the same ship after half of the planks are replaced? What about after they are all replaced?

Thomas Hobbes, whom we met in the previous chapter, made the question even harder by supposing that, as the planks are removed, they are reassembled into another ship. Once all of Theseus' planks are replaced, we have two ships: an old ship made of new planks and a new ship made of old planks! Which ship is the ship of Theseus?

The problem of personal identity

While this question can apply to any object, it becomes particularly disturbing applied to yourself. When you look at your baby pictures, you say 'That's me!' and your relatives describe how you were as a baby. But was that little creature really you? You've changed so much in so many ways.

How does a human being remain the same person throughout their life? This is known as the **problem of personal identity**.

Speaking in purely physical terms, it's hard to see how you can claim to be the same person as the baby in the pictures. The cells in your body don't last. After an average of seven years, they are entirely replaced (with the exception of a handful of brain cells). Physically, you are not made of the same material as you were – and you certainly don't look the same as you did.

Of course, a dualist, like Descartes, whom we met in Chapter 5, claims that human beings have souls. Could your soul be what makes you the same as the baby in the picture?

Once again, it's hard to see how. The soul is the thinking and feeling part of the self. It's absurd to suppose that a baby has the same kinds of thoughts and feelings as a grown adult. In fact, if you can remember some of the things you thought and felt as a small child, then you know how very different you were in those days. If there is such a thing as the soul, it seems that it changes just as much as the body does.

Amid all of this change, what stays the same? Is there an enduring self?

The memory criterion

The English philosopher John Locke (1632–1704) was worried about this problem because he wanted to believe in life after death. According to standard Christian theology, human beings receive a new body when they die and go to heaven. Locke was wondering whether and how his new heavenly self would be the same as his old earthly self.

He began thought-experimenting. What if the soul of a prince were transplanted into the body of a cobbler? Would the result be a prince or a cobbler?

Locke thinks the answer is clear: the result – let's call him George – would still be a prince. Imagine being George. It would feel strange suddenly to find yourself in a new body so different from the one you were used to. And yet, in the end, it wouldn't be very different from changing clothes. Would you go out and start cobbling? Of course not – you wouldn't even know how! All you could do is try to carry on with the life you remembered.

For Locke, this thought experiment reveals the source of personal identity: memory. Locke presents this view, which has come to be known as the **memory criterion of personal identity**, in the following passage.

> *For as far as any intelligent being can repeat the idea of any past action with the same consciousness it had of it at first, and with the same consciousness it has of any present action; so far it is the same personal self. For it is by the consciousness it has of its present thoughts and actions, that it is self to itself now, and so will be the same self, as far as the same consciousness can extend to actions past or to come, and would be by distance of time, or change of substance, no more two persons, than a man be two men by wearing other clothes to-day than he did yesterday, with a long or a short sleep between: the same consciousness uniting those distant actions into the same person, whatever substances contributed to their production.*
> John Locke, *Of Identity and Diversity*, ed. Jack Lynch (http://andromeda.rutgers.edu/~jlynch/Texts/locke227html)

When you think about yourself you remember your past. The memory of what you have done is what makes those actions yours instead of someone else's. It makes you the same person as you were then, despite all your physical and mental changes.

Consciousness is self-aware mental activity. Dualists believe this activity occurs in the soul while materialists insist that there is no need for the soul because consciousness can occur in the brain. Locke's point is that it doesn't matter where consciousness occurs – it is the source of our enduring sense of self.

Personal responsibility

The advantage of linking personhood with consciousness is that consciousness can then be transferred to a new body or even to a new soul while preserving the person.

In the opening thought experiment of this chapter, we considered a series of operations that would replace your entire body. Locke would allow this, and would even allow cases in which your consciousness is transferred into an animal, an alien life form, or an artificial life form such as a robot. While no longer being the same man or woman, you would still be the same person, in Locke's view, insofar as you could remember your preceding life.

Locke developed this solution in order to make sense of reward and punishment, both human and divine. He believed that, when you reach the afterlife, you will remember all that you did on earth, and so you will understand and deserve the reward or punishment you receive. The same goes for human justice. For example, you may not remember what you did while you were drunk, but you surely remember your decision to drink, and this is what you will be held responsible for.

If consciousness is what gives us unity as persons, then what happens when we lose consciousness, such as during sleep or after a head injury?

Locke is content to grant that we are not quite ourselves in such cases. Periods of unconsciousness are interruptions in our lives, not as human beings, but as persons. He is also content to grant that our lives as persons don't exactly begin at birth – insofar as infants are neither self-aware nor do they remember the past. You become a person slowly, as you mature.

And there's no doubt that people mature at different rates. Take a moment right now to think about your earliest memories… This is when you became a person. You are now the same person as you were then, as long as you can access the same consciousness in the form of a memory.

Locke's memory criterion may help to explain our ambivalent attitude towards children. As human beings, they are legally protected. Nevertheless, we grant them limited rights and responsibilities because they are not fully persons until their consciousness matures. It is the same for the elderly: as our memories fade with the onset of senility, so too does our personhood, while leaving our humanity intact.

> *Gentlemen, it is a fact that every philosopher of eminence for the last two centuries has either been murdered, or, at the least, been very near it, insomuch that if a man calls himself a philosopher, and never had his life attempted, rest assured there is nothing in him; and against Locke's philosophy in particular, I think it is an unanswerable objection (if we needed any) that, although he carried his throat about him in this world for seventy-two years, no man ever condescended to cut it.*
> Thomas De Quincey, 'Murder Considered as One of the Fine Arts' (1827)

Empiricism

Although Locke rejected Hobbes's materialism in favour of Descartes's dualism, he did not follow a rationalist epistemology. On the contrary, he explicitly argues against the doctrine of innate ideas, advancing one of the strongest statements of empiricism on record.

> *Let us then suppose the mind to be, as we say, white paper, void of all characters, without any ideas: How comes it to be furnished? Whence comes it by that vast store which the busy and boundless fancy of man has painted on it with an almost endless variety? Whence has it all the materials of reason and knowledge? To this I answer, in one word, from EXPERIENCE. In that all our knowledge is founded; and from that it ultimately derives itself. Our observation employed either, about external sensible objects, or about the internal operations of our minds perceived and reflected on by ourselves, is that which supplies our understandings with all the materials of thinking. These two are the fountains of knowledge, from whence all the ideas we have, or can naturally have, do spring.*
>
> John Locke, *An Essay Concerning Human Understanding* (http://oregonstate.edu/instruct/phl302/texts/locke/locke1/Book2a.html#Chapter%20I)

Aristotle, whom we met in Chapter 2, would agree, as would many philosophers today. The theory that human beings are born 'white paper' without any ideas has come to be known as the **tabula rasa theory** (from the Latin for 'blank slate'). It carries many political and psychological implications and is not without controversy.

Primary and secondary qualities

The main challenge facing empiricists concerns reliability. Recall that Descartes and Plato were pushed to posit an internal source of knowledge because they felt they could not trust their senses.

Consider, for example, the litmus test often taken in high-school physics classes. Each student is given a piece of the same paper and told to place it on their tongue. To some, the paper tastes bitter; to others, it has no taste at all. So, is the paper really bitter or not? Which students are deceived by their senses?

Case study: Locke and political liberalism

For Locke, the thesis that human beings are born blank slates implies that we are born free and equal, a thesis that led him to develop a groundbreaking political theory. Having read the work of Hobbes, Locke was determined to show that social contract theory need not lead to absolute sovereignty.

Like Rousseau, Locke starts with a more optimistic picture of human behaviour in the state of nature. Although we wouldn't constantly be at one another's throats without government, in Locke's view we would have plenty of occasions for disagreement over one thing in particular: property.

What is property? What does someone have a right to claim as their own – and why? This question cuts right to the core of human social relations. It may not occur to us to ask this question when we are accustomed to dealing only with property transference. That is, it seems obvious that, if you own something, and you give it or sell it to me, then I have the right to claim it as my own. But how did you (or whoever transferred it to you) come to own it in the first place? If you are the first to discover a stretch of land, for example, do you have the right to claim it?

Locke argues that we become rightful owners of something by mixing our labour with it. Clearly, you own your own labour. So, if you make a stretch of unclaimed land into a farm, then you can rightfully call that farm your own. This thesis represented a revolutionary departure from divine or royal conceptions of property and continues to provide a model for rightful ownership today.

In Locke's view, we consent to government only in order to secure an impartial judge to prevent and resolve property disputes. By conceiving of human social relations in terms of innate freedom and equality, Locke became the founding father of political liberalism. His threefold civic formula of 'life, liberty and property' influenced the United States Declaration of Independence, which famously guarantees 'life, liberty, and the pursuit of happiness'.

The same kind of disagreement turns up for so many other sensations. If the five senses give different data to different people, how can they be regarded as a reliable source of knowledge?

Locke sets out to show that the problem of sensory reliability can be solved by distinguishing between two different types of qualities. **Primary qualities,** which include size ('extension'), shape ('figure'), quantity ('number') and motion, are objective because they really exist in the objects. **Secondary qualities,** which include colour, smell, taste and sound, are subjective, because they exist only in our minds.

It may seem surprising at first to hear Locke assert that a sensation like colour doesn't really exist. On closer examination, however, it seems he may be right. What is the colour yellow? It is a certain wavelength of light reflecting off an object. Because a wavelength of light has a certain size, shape, quantity and extension, it really exists (it is a primary quality in Locke's terms). The yellowness, however, is just your eye's interpretation of that wavelength.

It's the same for sound. Locke's answer to the famous philosophical question: if a tree falls in the forest and no one is there to hear it, does it make a sound? is 'no'. A falling tree creates a disturbance in the air (a primary quality) that becomes a sound (a secondary quality) only for those who have ears. The same goes for taste and smell. These secondary qualities are mental interpretations of primary qualities.

Spotlight

A philosophy professor walks in to give his class their final exam. Placing his chair on his desk, he says, 'Using every applicable thing you've learned in this course, prove to me that this chair DOES NOT EXIST.' Pencils fly furiously as the students embark on long, complicated novels. One student, however, spends just 30 seconds writing his answer and then turns it in – to the astonishment of his peers. The professor takes one glance at the exam and gives it an A. The student's answer to the question: 'What chair?'

Locke asserts that only the subjective aspect of sensation is unreliable. Primary qualities are reliable because they are objectively measurable. For example, with the litmus test, we need simply show that there are molecules of a certain size and shape on the paper. The fact that this primary quality is interpreted as bitter to some and not to others need not concern us at all. Or so Locke thought...

Berkeley's slippery slope

George Berkeley (1685–1753) was an eighteenth-century Irish bishop who read Locke's works enthusiastically, wanting to be an empiricist. He found, however, that Locke's distinction between primary and secondary qualities becomes a slippery slope that leads straight into idealism, the view we met in Chapter 1, according to which the material world around us is not real.

Berkeley discovered that the very same arguments Locke uses to show that secondary qualities are subjective apply in the same way to primary qualities. Therefore all qualities are subjective, and nothing really exists outside the mind!

Now, if it be certain that those original qualities [i.e., primary qualities] are inseparably united with the other sensible qualities [i.e. secondary qualities], and not, even in thought, capable of being abstracted from them, it plainly follows that they exist only in the mind. But I desire any one to reflect and try whether he can, by any abstraction of thought, conceive the extension and motion of a body without all other sensible qualities. For my own part, I see evidently that it is not in my power to frame an idea of a body extended and moving, but I must withal give it some colour or other sensible quality which is acknowledged to exist only in the mind. In short, extension, figure, and motion, abstracted from all other qualities, are inconceivable. Where therefore the other sensible qualities are, there must these be also, to wit, in the mind and nowhere else.

George Berkeley, *Of the Principles of Human Knowledge* (http://www.marxists.org/reference/subject/philosophy/works/en/berkeley.htm)

Berkeley reasons syllogistically that, if wavelength 570–590 nm is yellow, and yellow is subjective, then wavelength 570–590 nm must be subjective as well.

Berkeley was rather eccentric for a bishop, because he actually came to believe that the world does not exist. He figured it would be much more efficient for God to transmit the idea of the world to our minds without bothering to create matter. (Descartes, in contrast, as we saw in Chapter 5, would regard this as an intolerable deception, of which a benevolent deity would be incapable.)

Philosophers continue to regard Berkeley as an important part of the history of philosophy, not necessarily because they agree with his idealist conclusion, but because he put his finger on a real problem with pure empiricism. Perhaps the only solution is to find a way to combine it with rationalism, as we shall see Kant attempting, in Chapter 9.

Spotlight

Overheard in eighteenth-century Ireland: 'Did you hear that George Berkeley died? His girlfriend stopped seeing him.'

Key ideas

Idealism: The view that the material world around us is not real
Memory criterion of personal identity: Consciousness of the past makes you the same person as you were then, despite all your physical and mental changes
Political liberalism: A limited conception of government based on liberty and equality
Primary qualities: Objective qualities that really exist in the objects
Problem of personal identity: How does a human being remain the same person throughout their life?
Secondary qualities: Subjective qualities that exist only in our minds
Ship of Theseus thought experiment: If all of a ship's planks are replaced one by one, does it remain the same ship?
Tabula rasa: Latin for 'blank slate'; the theory that human beings are born without any innate ideas

Fact-check

1 According to Locke, the sensation of taste is which of the following?
  a A primary quality
  b A secondary quality
  c An objective quality
  d A substantial quality

2 Locke thinks that, when we sleep, we are not...
  a Persons
  b Human beings
  c Really existing
  d Really alive

3 Which of the following is central to political liberalism?
  a Absolute sovereignty
  b Idealism
  c Memory
  d Equality

4 What does it mean to say that Locke's distinction between primary and secondary qualities is a 'slippery slope'?
  a It is surprisingly hard to understand
  b It contains hidden contradictions
  c It disguises other, more controversial, claims
  d It leads to something Locke did not intend

5 Which of the following raises the problem of personal identity?
  a Alzheimer's disease
  b An 'antique' clock with new parts
  c Tone deafness
  d Colour blindness

6 Suppose Joe and Arlene can't remember making their wedding vows. Which of the following would Locke be most likely to say?
  a They're no longer married because they're no longer the same persons
  b They're still married because they're still the same human beings

   c They're no longer married because they're no longer the same human beings

   d They're still married because they're still the same persons

7 Which of the following views does Berkeley endorse?
   a Empiricism
   b Idealism
   c Materialism
   d Dualism

8 Which of the following would have the most legitimate claim to own a cave at the bottom of the ocean, according to Locke?
   a The person who first discovered it
   b The country nearest to it
   c The people who make it into a tourist attraction
   d The people who know most about ocean caves

9 On which of the following grounds does Berkeley argue that primary qualities exist only in the mind?
   a They can't be conceived without secondary qualities
   b They are less reliable than secondary qualities
   c They are more reliable than secondary qualities
   d They are never accompanied by secondary qualities

10 Where does all knowledge come from, according to Locke?
   a Experience
   b Reason
   c Perception
   d Ideas

Dig deeper

Nicholas Jolley, *Locke: His Philosophical Thought* (Oxford University Press, 1999)

Galen Strawson, *Locke on Personal Identity* (Princeton University Press, 2011)

William Uzgalis, *Locke's Essay Concerning Human Understanding: A Reader's Guide* (Continuum, 2007)

Hume and causality

'A wise man proportions his belief to the evidence.'
David Hume

In this chapter you will learn:

▶ *about the problem of induction*
▶ *why Hume questions the laws of nature*
▶ *the connection between repetition and causation*
▶ *why Hume thinks empiricism requires scepticism*
▶ *how Leibniz and Spinoza use theism to secure the laws of nature*
▶ *Hume's distinction between logical truths and observed truths*
▶ *why Hume rejects miracles as well as the existence of an enduring self.*

Thought experiment: miracle pool

It's Friday night. You're heading down to your favourite watering hole to have a drink and shoot some pool. When you arrive you note with displeasure that someone you don't know has already commandeered the pool table. It's a large man in an odd, reddish hat. He feels your gaze as you pass to the bar and looks up.

'I'm just getting started,' he says. 'Would you like to join me?'

You shrug and nod. Drinks are bought, introductions are made, and the balls are racked.

He breaks and it's an open table.

'The three in that corner,' you call, leaning in for an easy shot.

David holds up his hand. 'What makes you say that?'

You pause and smile uncertainly. Is he making a joke? When he says nothing further, you take your shot.

The cue ball rolls fast up to the three. Upon contact, however, it comes to an instant halt without budging the three at all. The two balls remain at absolute rest.

'What the hell?' you complain. 'Something's wrong with the table.' You reach for the cue ball, pick it up and shake it, while sliding your other hand over the green material on the table.

'Why do you think something's wrong?' David asks.

'Are you kidding me? This ball just defied the laws of physics...'

'What a strange thing to say,' David remarks. 'Inanimate objects aren't capable of defying or obeying any laws...' He plucks the cue ball from your hand, placing it back on the table where it had stopped. 'Nine in the side.'

You stare at him uncomprehendingly. Not only is he completely unconcerned about the behaviour of the cue ball, he has just called an impossible shot.

'The nine in this pocket?' you interject.

'Yes.'

'But that would be a miracle!'

David wrinkles his brow in amusement and takes his shot. The cue ball rolls to the nine. Then, barely making contact, and without budging the nine, it reverses and rolls back to where it started.

You gape. He shrugs.

You look around, expecting someone to jump out of the shadows and yell 'April Fool!' No one does. You peer into your drink and take a whiff, wondering if someone slipped you a hallucinogen.

'How'd you rig the balls?' you ask, reaching for the nine. But he blocks your hand.

'Just take your turn, will you?'

'Well, fine,' you mutter. 'Why not? But I'm not putting any money on this game.' You scan the table and then point. 'The seven in that corner.'

You bend low, aiming carefully for a long shot. The cue ball rolls fast up to the seven. Upon contact, the seven stays at absolute rest while the cue ball leaps off the table and flies towards David, smacking into him hard, right between the eyes. He falls backward against some chairs and tumbles noisily to the ground.

People sitting at the bar turn and gasp. The bartender throws down his rag and storms angrily towards you...

That wasn't supposed to happen

We've all made predictions that turned out to be wrong. When this happens, we typically discover some hidden factor, which, if known, would have enabled us to make the right prediction. The world is very predictable.

And it's a good thing, because we count on it.

Imagine how hard it would be to carry on with your life if you weren't sure whether the sun would rise tomorrow or whether gravity would hold.

The world behaves in such a predicable way that scientists codify its behaviour in terms of 'laws': 'For every action, there is an equal and opposite reaction' and so on. You probably learned several of these laws in your school physics lessons and 'proved' them using various projectiles. Well, leave it to philosophers to question what everyone else takes for granted as common knowledge.

The notion of a law implies necessity. When we learn the laws of physics we come to believe that objects behave as they do because they have to. Upon closer examination, however, it cannot be denied that there is a gap between the following two statements:

> Things always behave this way.

> Things have to behave this way.

To see the gap, all you have to do is think of something you always do, such as have a morning cup of coffee. Suppose you have had a cup of coffee every morning for the past 100 years. Does that mean you have to have a cup of coffee this morning?

Of course not. In fact, human beings behave in surprising ways far more often than do inanimate objects, which is what leads some people to believe in free will, as discussed in Chapter 6. Setting aside the question of free will, the coffee example shows, at least, that repetition is not the same as necessity.

The problem of induction

The Scottish philosopher David Hume (1711–76) was the first to point this out. He made a revolutionary impact on the history of Western civilization with a single assertion:

> The future may not be like the past.

On the surface, this assertion seems so obvious. Of course the future could be different! Who expects it to be the same?

But everyone does, including you. You expect the sun to rise, you expect gravity to hold, and you expect the action of every billiard ball to have an equal and opposite reaction.

To show that these expectations are unwarranted, Hume presents a thought experiment about billiard balls, as in the opening of this chapter. Granted that, in the past, every action has met with an equal and opposite reaction, Hume asks: how do you know this will hold in the future? What's to stop a billiard ball from behaving in a completely new way?

> *When I see, for instance, a billiard-ball moving in a straight line towards another; even suppose motion in the second ball should by accident be suggested to me, as the result of their contact or impulse; may I not conceive, that a hundred different events might as well follow from that cause? May not both these balls remain at absolute rest? May not the first ball return in a straight line, or leap off from the second in any line or direction? All these suppositions are consistent and conceivable. Why then should we give the preference to one, which is no more consistent or conceivable than the rest? All our reasonings a priori will never be able to show us any foundation for this preference.*
>
> David Hume, *An Enquiry Concerning Human Understanding* (http://web. mnstate.edu/gracyk/courses/web%20publishing/enquiryIVi.htm)

You claim to know how that billiard ball will behave. But how will you justify this claim? How will you explain your confidence about the future in general? This is known as the **problem of induction,** because induction is the logic we use in drawing a general conclusion from particular instances.

Spotlight

Einstein would never have dared to question the physics of Newton if it weren't for Hume. In a letter to a friend, Einstein wrote that he read Hume's *Treatise* 'with eagerness and admiration' shortly before discovering relativity theory.

What is a cause?

People speak confidently about one thing 'causing' another as though they have seen causation with their own eyes. In fact, no one has ever seen causation itself. What we have seen is various events occurring in succession.

Sometimes, when one event succeeds another we make no special connection between the two. For example, suppose a leaf falls from a tree and then a ladybird lands on it. You wouldn't say that the falling of the leaf caused the ladybird to land on it. The two events occurred together only once – there was no connection between them.

At other times, when one event succeeds another we make a special connection between the two. Consider the following succession of events:

> One billiard ball moves across the table, makes contact with another, and then the other ball continues across the table. One billiard ball moves across the table, makes contact with another, and then the other ball continues across the table. One billiard ball moves across the table, makes contact with another, and then the other ball continues across the table. One billiard ball moves across the table, makes contact with another, and then the other ball continues across the table...

We've seen this succession of events (and others just like it) so many times that we come to believe it cannot happen any differently. We say that the motion of the first ball 'causes' the motion of the second.

If we saw the behaviour of the billiard balls just once, it wouldn't occur to us to expect it to happen again. Nothing in the two motions themselves suggests necessity. The repetition, however – what Hume calls the 'constant conjunction' of events – leads us to believe that it has to happen every time.

It appears, then, that this idea of a necessary connexion among events arises from a number of similar instances which occur of the constant conjunction of these events; nor can that idea ever be suggested by any one of these instances, surveyed in all possible lights and positions. But there is nothing in a number of instances, different from every single instance, which is supposed to be exactly similar; except only, that after a repetition

> *of similar instances, the mind is carried by habit, upon the*
> *appearance of one event, to expect its usual attendant, and to*
> *believe that it will exist. This connexion, therefore, which we feel*
> *in the mind, this customary transition of the imagination from*
> *one object to its usual attendant, is the sentiment or impression*
> *from which we form the idea of power or necessary connexion.*
> *Nothing farther is in the case. Contemplate the subject on all*
> *sides; you will never find any other origin of that idea.*
>
> David Hume, *An Enquiry Concerning Human Understanding* (http://www.
> bartleby.com/37/3/10html)

Hume insists that causation, the 'necessary connection between events' is all in the mind, not in the world.

Have you contemplated it on all sides? Has Hume convinced you? Or do you still believe there are hidden mechanisms in the universe guaranteeing the connection between events?

A rationalist, who believes in the existence of things unseen, has the right to believe in hidden mechanisms. But an empiricist has no such right. Empiricists believe only what they experience. No one has ever experienced such mechanisms. And no one has ever experienced the future. So no one can claim to have any knowledge of how things will behave then.

Hume is an empiricist. His goal is to show that true empiricism requires a lot more scepticism, the attitude of doubt or disbelief, than people realize.

Spotlight

Have you seen Hume's missing shade of blue? As an empiricist, Hume says all ideas are copies of what we perceive. Yet we can have an idea of a shade of blue we have never seen that lies on the spectrum between two shades we have seen. How is this possible unless we have an inner source of ideas?

Case study: rationalists vs. empiricists

The authors we have examined so far in this book have been lining up on either side of the epistemological divide: Plato, Anselm and Descartes the rationalists; Aristotle, Aquinas, Hobbes, Locke, Berkeley and Hume the empiricists.

Baruch Spinoza (1632–77) and Gottfried Wilhelm von Leibniz (1646–1716) are two seventeenth-century philosophers who earned a place on the rationalist side. They weigh in on the problem of induction in an interesting way.

Leibniz argues that the laws of physics guarantee causal connections because they are based on the necessary natures of things. So, for a billiard ball to be a physical object is for it to act with an equal and opposite reaction. If it didn't, it wouldn't be what it is. And physical objects have to be what they are, in Leibniz's view, because they were made by God. As the best of all possible beings, God must create the best of all possible worlds. God gave physical objects the nature he did because this is the best possible nature they can have. Therefore, their predictable behaviour is necessary.

Spinoza regards the behaviour of the billiard ball as equally necessary, but for a different reason. In Spinoza's view, the infinity of God implies that God is everything. According to this philosophical pantheism, all of nature, including every physical object, is part of God. But God's infinity also implies that he must do exactly as he does – there is no left over room, so to speak, for him to do any differently. Therefore, all physical objects act with the same necessity.

In the end, theism guarantees the laws of physics for both Leibniz and Spinoza. Having barred theism from scientific reasoning on the grounds that theism involves things unseen, Hume is left without any such guarantee.

Relations of ideas vs. matters of fact

Hume supports his scepticism by arguing that all our experience produces knowledge that can be divided into two different categories.

1 **Relations of ideas** are logical truths, such as 'two plus two equals four'. These are necessary because the attempt to deny them results in a contradiction. If two plus two equalled five, then one plus one plus one plus one is not one plus one plus one plus one, which is a contradiction.

2 **Matters of fact** are observed truths, such as 'bread nourishes'. These are contingent (meaning 'not necessary') because you can deny them without producing a contradiction. The idea of bread poisoning instead of nourishing involves no conceptual impossibility. We can prove this by imagining a world where bread poisons instead of nourishes.

Hume points out that the assertion 'A causes B' is a matter of fact, not a relation of ideas. Therefore it can't be necessary.

Of course, everyone recognizes instances when matters of fact go differently from usual. We've all eaten something that usually nourishes us, only to find that, this time, it made us sick. When this happens, we are liable to look for a hidden cause – some microscopic bacteria in the food that gave us food poisoning.

But when Hume calls the nourishing effect of bread a matter of fact, he isn't saying that there may be hidden causes that make things turn out differently this time. He's saying that the bread could suddenly have a completely different effect without any different causes at all.

To insist that there would have to be different cause in order to produce a different effect would be to cast the nourishing effect of bread as a relation of ideas like 'two plus two equals four'. Because human beings are creatures of habit, we constantly view causal connections as logical connections. But this is a conceptual confusion we must overcome, in Hume's view.

It's not as though Hume recommends that we begin each day without any expectation of bread nourishing, the sun rising or gravity holding. In our daily lives we can continue to expect the succession of events we have grown so accustomed to. But by applying scepticism towards all things unseen, including the supposed 'laws of nature', we will think more clearly and be less likely to develop a mistaken understanding of the world.

Miracles

Ironically, Hume's rejection of causal necessity did not make him any more inclined to accept the occurrence of miracles. In fact, he felt that religion as a whole, which is largely based on miracles, presents a mistaken understanding of the world.

Hume defines a miracle as 'a transgression of a law of nature by a particular volition of the Deity, or by the interposition of some invisible agent'.

It may seem strange to hear Hume speak of 'laws of nature' after seeing him argue so vigorously against their existence. But, naturally, Hume doesn't want to deprive scientists of a very useful way of speaking about the causal patterns we've experienced. He simply redefines the idea of a law of nature as a codified description of the past behaviour of physical objects.

So a miracle is a supernatural break in the usual causal pattern we've experienced. Hume uses the strong language of 'transgression' because, while rejecting causal necessity, he still takes experience very seriously. Recall that, for an empiricist, experience is the basis of all our reasonable belief. And a miracle violates the expectations we form on the basis of experience. Thus, it cannot be reasonably believed.

Suppose someone claims to have witnessed a man raised from the dead. Hume asks us to consider how many times we have ever experienced such a thing occurring. He then asks us to consider how many times we have ever experienced someone lying to us or being mistaken about something they tell us. We should then decide to believe whichever we have experienced more often. While it isn't impossible for this decision to be wrong, it isn't reasonable to base our beliefs on anything else.

Hume offers a thought experiment to support his argument. Imagine an Indian prince who refuses to believe that water can freeze because he grew up in a hot country where he was never able to witness such an event occurring. The prince is reasoning correctly in Hume's view, because he is following empiricist principles. The prince would need to gain a good amount of experience with freezing water before believing in it.

While at first it may seem that Hume's denial of causal necessity should leave him especially open to miracles, on closer examination we see that his underlying scepticism provides a basis for questioning both causal necessity and miracles. It provides a basis for questioning many other things as well.

The bundle theory of personal identity

Hume did not believe in life after death. Such an occurrence would be a miracle, after all, and an anchor for the religious world view that he found so contrary to sound empirical thinking. Freed from religious motives, Hume's investigation of the question of how the self endures led to radical results.

We saw in the previous chapter how Locke's belief in life after death led him to the memory criterion of personal identity. Seeing problems with the endurance of both the body and the soul, Locke concluded that our consciousness is what endures – in the form of memory.

Hume was intrigued by the idea that an enduring consciousness is introspectively observable. As an empiricist, after all, Locke would not be entitled to believe he had an enduring consciousness at all unless he experienced it. Evidently, Locke was convinced that he did experience his self when he thought about his own thinking – remembering the experiences he has over time.

Hume, however, denies that reflection upon current or past experiences adds up to anything more than a bundle of perceptions. Hume's claim that what we call our 'self' is really nothing but a series of particular experiences has come to be known as the **bundle theory of personal identity**.

How extraordinary for Hume to conclude that he has no enduring self! And yet, if you take a moment to reflect on your own thinking, you may be hard pressed to disagree.

> *For my part, when I enter most intimately into what I call myself, I always stumble on some particular perception or other, of heat or cold, light or shade, love or hatred, pain or pleasure. I never can catch myself at any time without a perception, and never can observe any thing but the perception. When my perceptions are removed for any time, as by sound sleep, so long am I insensible of myself, and may truly be said not to exist. And were all my perceptions removed by death, and could I neither think, nor feel, nor see, nor love, nor hate, after the dissolution of my body, I should be entirely annihilated, nor do I conceive what is further requisite to make me a perfect nonentity. If anyone, upon serious and unprejudiced reflection, thinks he has a different notion of himself, I must confess I can reason no longer with him. All I can allow him is, that he may be in the right as well as I, and that we are essentially different in this particular. He may, perhaps, perceive something simple and continued, which he calls himself; though I am certain there is no such principle in me.*
>
> David Hume, *A Treatise of Human Nature* (http://andromeda.rutgers. edu/~jlynch/Texts/treatise.html)

Locke claimed that, when he remembered the past, he accessed the same consciousness as he had at that time. Is it really the same? When you remember the day you graduated from high school, for example, do you have the same consciousness as you had then, or just a similar one? Does it need to be the same in order for you to be the same person as that high-school student? These questions remain unresolved.

Key ideas

Bundle theory of personal identity: That what we call our 'self' is really nothing but some particular experience or other

Causation: The necessary connection between events

Constant conjunction: The repetition of events that gives rise to the idea of causal necessity

Matters of fact: Observed truths, such as 'bread nourishes'

Miracle: A transgression of a law of nature by a particular volition of the deity, or by the interposition of some invisible agent

Pantheism: That all of nature, including every physical object, is part of God

Problem of induction: How do we justify our claim to know how things will behave in the future?

Relations of ideas: Logical truths, such as 'two plus two equals four'

Scepticism: The attitude of doubt or disbelief

Fact-check

1 Which of the following does Hume observe when he introspects?
   a His self
   b Particular perceptions
   c His soul
   d God

2 For Hume, the idea of a necessary connection among events arises from which of the following?
   a Constant conjunction
   b Consciousness
   c Matters of fact
   d Relations of ideas

3 Suppose a scientist was speaking about the law of gravity. In which of the following ways would Hume be most likely to respond?
   a He would warn that the law of gravity does not exist
   b He would interpret the law of gravity as a record of past experience
   c He would infer that gravity will hold in the same way in the future
   d He would complain that he doesn't understand what the scientist means

4 Which of the following is entitled to believe in laws of nature?
   a Empiricists
   b Rationalists
   c Materialists
   d Idealists

5 Which of the following provides the foundation for Hume's philosophy?
   a Religion
   b Rationalism
   c Billiards
   d Scepticism

6 For Spinoza, causal necessity is implied by which of the following?
- **a** God's infinity
- **b** God's perfection
- **c** Human imagination
- **d** The constant conjunction of events

7 Which of the following is a reported miracle likely to be, according to Hume?
- **a** A lie
- **b** A transgression of the laws of nature
- **c** A matter of fact
- **d** A hidden mechanism

8 Which of the following does Hume deem necessary?
- **a** The laws of nature
- **b** Causal connection
- **c** Matters of fact
- **d** Relations of ideas

9 Which of the following is a matter of fact, in Hume's view?
- **a** That we perceive the self when we introspect
- **b** That no one has experienced the future
- **c** That two plus two equals four
- **d** That fire burns

10 Why is induction a problem?
- **a** Because no one knows what it really means
- **b** Because it defies the laws of nature
- **c** Because it is hard to justify the inference
- **d** Because no one has ever experienced a miracle

Dig deeper

Paul Stanistreet, *Hume's Scepticism and the Science of Human Nature* (Ashgate, 2002)

Saul Traiger, *The Blackwell Guide to Hume's Treatise* (Blackwell, 2006)

John P. Wright, *The Sceptical Realism of David Hume* (University of Minnesota Press, 1983)

9

Kant and duty

'Good will shines forth like a precious jewel.'
Immanuel Kant

In this chapter you will learn:

▶ *why Kant thinks it is always wrong to lie*
▶ *how Kant reconciles rationalism and empiricism*
▶ *about transcendental idealism, Kant's revolutionary thesis*
▶ *the meaning of Kant's categorical imperative*
▶ *how relativism opposes ethics*
▶ *what it means to treat people as ends in themselves*
▶ *the significance of good will for Kant's deontology.*

Thought experiment: the trouble with Harry

Your sweet, funny, little old granny has finally succumbed to the unkind effects of age. Puttering in her garden, she fell and broke her hip. She lies in hospital right now with multiplying complications. There's nothing the doctors can do; they give her a week at most.

Sweet, funny, little old Granny has a gigantic, foul-smelling, obnoxious mutt of a dog named Harry. When Granny was admitted to the hospital, the great majority of her distress was not for herself but for her dog: who would take care of him? You, of course, assured Granny that you would take Harry home and treat him like a king.

That was the beginning of a great war that ended in tragedy. After fighting with Harry over everything from where to poop, to how early in the morning to start barking, to whether the living-room curtains are fair game for dinner, you felt desperate to be rid of him. Nevertheless, you sincerely did not intend to leave the gate unlatched, enabling him to get out while you were away at work. He ran out into traffic and was flattened almost beyond recognition.

To make matters worse, he badly damaged the Mercedes convertible that hit him, leaving its driver with a deep cut on her face and a bad case of whiplash. Before the ambulance took her away, she grilled concerned onlookers about the tagless dog's owner and swore she would sue.

You learned all this from your next-door neighbour when you happened to see him on your return from work this evening. No one knew about Harry's brief stay at your house. Your neighbour said the woman's lawyer has begun knocking on doors up and down the street to find out who was responsible for him.

Meanwhile, you're already late for your promised visit to Granny at the hospital. You pull out of your driveway and grip the steering wheel of your car with white knuckles as you picture what's going to happen next:

You walk into the hospital room and that dear woman turns her bedraggled head. Her fading eyes light up when she recognizes you. She reaches out for a hug. 'So nice of you to come, honey! Come and sit a spell! How are you? And how's my darlin' Harry?'

Three questions pound heavily through your mind:

1 When Granny insists on a report about her dog, will you tell her the truth?

2 When the victim's lawyer comes knocking on your door, will you tell him the truth?

3 At Granny's funeral, when the relatives ask what's to be done with her dog, will you tell them the truth?

Liar, liar, pants on fire!

How often do you lie? Do you lie about how often you lie?

The three questions at the end of the above thought experiment present three different kinds of lies.

▶ The first is a lie to someone you love for their sake. (You want to protect Granny from a hurtful truth that she doesn't need to know because she will never find out.)

▶ The second is a lie to someone you don't know for your own sake. (You want to protect yourself from the expense and hassle of a lawsuit provoked by your own negligence.)

▶ The third is a lie to someone you love for your own sake. (You want to protect yourself from the harsh judgement of your relatives.)

Be honest: would you be honest? Or would you find a way to 'justify' a little dishonesty?

While most people are probably happy to live with some amount of dishonesty in their lives, the German philosopher Immanuel Kant (1724–1804) is not. In his view, lying is always wrong: everywhere, any time, for anyone, no matter how painful the truth.

Kant's uncompromising position on honesty is a direct implication of his ethical theory, which is, in turn, a direct implication of his metaphysics, which is, in turn, a direct implication of his epistemology. While every philosopher tries to integrate all the elements of their philosophy, none is as systematic as Kant.

> *Two things fill the mind with ever new and increasing admiration and awe, the oftener and the more steadily we reflect on them: the starry heavens above and the moral law within. I have not to search for them and conjecture them as though they were veiled in darkness or were in the transcendent region beyond my horizon; I see them before me and connect them directly with the consciousness of my existence. The former begins from the place I occupy in the external world of sense, and enlarges my connection therein to an unbounded extent with worlds upon worlds and systems of systems, and moreover into limitless times of their periodic motion, its beginning and continuance. The second begins from my invisible self, my personality, and exhibits me in a world which has true infinity, but which is traceable only by the understanding, and with which I discern that I am not in a merely contingent but in a universal and necessary connection, as I am also thereby with all those visible worlds.*
>
> Immanuel Kant, *Critique of Practical Reason* (http://www.gutenberg.org/cache/epub/5683/pg5683html)

Kant was arguably the greatest systematizer of all time, building an extraordinarily complex theory of everything, full of so many long sentences and big words – many of which he made up – that it was guaranteed to remain at the centre of intellectual controversy to the present day and beyond.

Spotlight

Kant was an eccentric recluse who never left his home town and went on a walk with his butler at the same time every day. His neighbours used to say he was so punctual that they could set their clocks when they saw him pass. He forgot his walk only once – the day he read the work of Jean-Jacques Rousseau.

An epistemological compromise

Kant surveyed the debate between rationalists and empiricists and found it at an impasse – both sides seeking unsuccessfully to secure human knowledge.

Empiricists begin firmly grounded in experience of the physical world, but proceed to render the human mind a passive receptacle of data. Rationalists keep the human mind actively searching for the truth within, but leave us in doubt about the physical world.

Kant decided that the only solution is to combine the best components from each side. He begins with experience of the external world, but makes that experience essentially active rather than passive, so that we can confidently claim to know what we experience.

In order to explain this compromise, Kant introduces a new conceptual category, which is based on a combination of old categories. Recall that we encountered the following categories in Chapter 4:

a priori: knowledge that does not depend on experience

vs.

a posteriori: knowledge that depends on experience.

And we encountered the following categories in Chapter 7:

matters of fact: observed truths, such as 'bread nourishes'

vs.

relations of ideas: logical truths, such as 'two plus two equals four'.

You would think that relations of ideas are always a priori and matters of fact are always a posteriori. In fact, this was everyone's assumption before Kant arrived on the scene. Kant combines the a priori with matters of fact (which he calls 'synthetic') to create a new category of understanding which he calls the **a priori synthetic**.

Kant asserts that time and space, the two concepts that together define the physical world, are a priori synthetic concepts. This means that our knowledge of time and space does not depend on experience, even though it shapes that very experience and makes it possible for us to perceive objects in the world.

Transcendental idealism

If our knowledge of time and space does not depend on experience, where does it come from?

It comes from within our minds.

Kant asserts that time and space are concepts that human beings impose on the physical world. They don't exist in the world but rather are the way in which the rational mind understands the world. If there were no rational minds, there would be no time or space.

What would the world be like without time or space?

No one knows. No one *can* know. It's impossible for us to conceive of the world except through these concepts.

Kant calls the physical world as it would be without the human concepts of time and space the **noumenal** realm, from the Greek word for 'thought'. The noumenal realm consists of things-in-themselves and transcends human experience.

Kant calls the physical world as perceived through the human concepts of time and space the **phenomenal** realm, from the Greek word for 'appearance'. The phenomenal realm consists of things-as-they-appear-to-us.

Kant is called a 'transcendental idealist' because, like Plato, the idealist whom we met in Chapter 2, he places ultimate reality in a realm beyond human experience. Against Plato, however, who concluded that the physical world is an illusion, Kant insists that the phenomenal realm is real for us. When rational beings apply the categories of time and space to their experiences they help to construct the world.

Deontology

Constructing the world may sound like a highly creative process, but, in fact, Kant thinks rationality imposes strict necessity on it. For example, if you are perceiving the world in a rational way, then every billiard ball must have an equal and opposite reaction.

But Kant isn't solely or even primarily interested in the laws of physics. He wants to argue that, just as our concepts of time and space necessitate our experience, so also does our concept of duty. If you're thinking rationally, then you must act in accordance with the moral law.

Since Kant's ethics holds that rational beings discover the moral law within themselves in the form of duty, it is called **deontology** from the Greek word for 'duty'.

The categorical imperative (first formulation)

The dictates of duty are not only necessary, they are universal, meaning that they are the same for everyone at all times. Since duty tells human beings what they must do by virtue of their rationality, and all human beings are rational by nature, we will all be subject to the very same moral requirements.

Kant points out that many people make the mistake of thinking of duty in the form of hypothetical imperatives. For example:

'If you want to have friends, then you must be kind.'

Any such 'If ... then' statement premises moral obligation (kindness) upon a desired outcome (having friends). Such an imperative cannot be ethical because you only need to deny the 'if' part to escape the obligation. If you don't want to have friends, then you don't need to be kind.

Kant argues that true duty can only be conceived of in the form of a categorical imperative – a requirement that leaves room for no 'ifs', 'ands' or 'buts'. For example:

'Be kind.'

Period. It doesn't matter what you want or need or feel. This is what is required of you as a rational being.

We could make a list of a great number of duties we are obligated to uphold. In Kant's view, however, all our duties can be captured in a single categorical imperative.

> *The categorical imperative alone has the purport of a practical law; all the rest may indeed be called principles of the will but not laws, since whatever is only necessary for the attainment of some arbitrary purpose may be considered as in itself contingent, and we can at any time be free from the precept if we give up the purpose; on the contrary, the unconditional command leaves the will no liberty to choose the opposite; consequently it alone carries with it that necessity which we require in a law. [...] There is therefore but one categorical imperative, namely, this: Act only on that maxim whereby thou canst at the same time will that it should become a universal law.*
>
> Immanuel Kant, *Groundwork for the Metaphysics of Morals* (http://ethics. sandiego.edu/Books/Kant/MM/Part2html)

When considering the morality of the proposed course of action (what Kant calls a maxim), we ask ourselves, what would happen if everybody did this? The categorical imperative requires that our actions be universalizable.

Case study: Ruth Benedict and relativism

Kant's deontology stands at the opposite end of the spectrum from relativism, according to which there are no universal moral truths.

The twentieth-century relativist Ruth Benedict (1887–1948) was an American anthropologist who travelled the world observing different cultures with different value systems. Some regard homosexuality as immoral; others don't. Some regard meat-eating as immoral; others don't. Some regard human sacrifice as immoral; others don't. Who's to say which of these values is right and which is wrong? Benedict concludes that all morality is relative to the culture to which you happen to belong. Her view became very popular at the end of the twentieth century because it seems to promote tolerance of diversity.

The problem with relativism is that the claim that 'there are no universal moral truths' is itself a moral value. Who's to say it is right? That is, by claiming that there is no legitimate way to make moral judgements, relativists deprive themselves of the ability to make any legitimate moral judgements. This is a self-contradiction, meaning the view has to be rejected or revised to avoid the contradiction somehow.

Most philosophers conclude that relativism is too extreme in its tolerance. The ethical views we're looking at in this book (Aristotle's virtue theory, Kant's deontology, Mill's utilitarianism) can all be interpreted in ways that are consistent with varying degrees of tolerance.

Applying the categorical imperative

Go back to the case of Granny and her dog, with which we began this chapter. What should you do? On Kant's view, you must ask yourself whether the following would be a good law:

> 'Everyone should always lie to protect themselves or others.'

Upon putting the issue in these terms, you may be thinking: 'Well, I wouldn't want to live in a world full of liars, and besides, there's no guarantee that the people I lie to won't find out…'

But it's crucial to realize that Kant's categorical imperative is not motivated by a concern about the possible consequences of the proposed action. That, after all, would render it a hypothetical imperative, such as:

> 'If you don't want to live in a world full of liars, then don't lie.'

or

> 'If you don't want to run the risk of being found out, then don't lie.'

These hypothetical imperatives enable you to escape your duty to be honest. All you have to do is decide you don't care about living with liars or running risks – then you are free to lie as much as you like.

That's not how Kant's ethics works.

For Kant, duty is rationally inescapable. The point of universalizing your maxim is to see whether it would even be possible for a fully rational agent to engage in the proposed course of action.

Rather amazingly, Kant insists that fully rational agents are incapable of committing immoral actions. This is to say that your noumenal self literally cannot lie. When you lie, you sink into your phenomenal self – you give up being a thing-in-itself and become a mere thing-as-it-appears.

Why is this?

Kant contends that every immoral act is self-contradictory. And fully rational agents cannot contradict themselves. Therefore, fully rational agents cannot commit immoral acts.

But how is lying self-contradictory?

Kant suggests that the very act of speaking presupposes honesty. That is, why would you make verbal sounds for me to hear unless there was an underlying assumption between us that you were trying to communicate something? When you lie you're not communicating but undermining communication. So your very act negates itself – a self-contradiction.

Kant thinks every immoral act is subject to the same sort of analysis. Critics assert, however, that it's hard to see any self-contradiction in many immoral acts.

For example, suppose you're taking a bus trip. The man sitting behind you starts speaking to his companion in a very annoying way. After an hour of unsuccessfully trying to ignore him, you have an overwhelming urge to clock him.

Clearly this would be wrong. But how is it self-contradictory?

The categorical imperative (second formulation)

Kant offers another formulation of his categorical imperative to help show how it applies. He says that that universalizing your proposed actions means always regarding others as ends in themselves, never as the means to an end.

By 'end in itself' Kant means something that's worth having for its own sake. For example, when a couple decides to have children, they should, and typically do, think of those children as ends in themselves. By contrast, it would be wrong to have children so that they could help out on the farm. This would be to treat the children as a means to the end of having a more productive farm. To treat someone as the means to an end is to use them. It's wrong to use people.

Kant would insist that whenever you lie to someone you're using them. You need them to be ignorant of the truth in order to accomplish your goal. Even if your goal may seem noble – such as protecting them or others from harm – the ends don't justify the means. Likewise, if you clock someone for being annoying, you're using them to relieve your frustration.

Kant thought we should all learn to put our own selfish goals aside, striving instead to bring about a 'kingdom of ends'.

Spotlight

Kant asserted that masturbation is a violation of the moral law, while admitting that it was hard to think of a good argument why.

Good will

> Nothing can possibly be conceived in the world, or even out of it, which can be called good, without qualification, except a good will. Intelligence, wit, judgement, and the other talents of the mind, however they may be named, or courage, resolution, perseverance, as qualities of temperament, are undoubtedly good and desirable in many respects; but these gifts of nature may also become extremely bad and mischievous if the will which is to make use of them, and which, therefore, constitutes what is called character, is not good. It is the same with the gifts of fortune. Power, riches, honour, even health, and the general well-being and contentment with one's condition which is called happiness, inspire pride, and often presumption, if there is not a good will to correct the influence of these on the mind, and with this also to rectify the whole principle of acting and adapt it to its end. The sight of a being who is not adorned with a single feature of a pure and good will, enjoying unbroken prosperity, can never give pleasure to an impartial rational spectator. Thus a good will appears to constitute the indispensable condition even of being worthy of happiness.
>
> Immanuel Kant, *Groundwork for the Metaphysics of Morals* (http://ethics. sandiego.edu/Books/Kant/MM/Part1html)

Kant points out that you should know what it is to treat someone as an end in itself because you are probably accustomed to treating yourself that way. Healthy people treat themselves as valuable for their own sakes.

Consequently, many of Kant's readers feel that, in the end, Kant's ethical theory really amounts to little more than the age-old wisdom found in many religions, including Christianity, known as the Golden Rule: 'Do unto others as you would have them do unto you.'

Though Kant was a Christian, he did not want to reduce his ethical theory to the Golden Rule. After all, it's easy enough to imagine someone who treats others as valuable for their own sake without actually regarding them as such. For example,

I might refrain from clocking you for annoying me while all the while despising you and wishing you were dead.

For Kant, this will not do at all. To regard others as ends in themselves is not just to act as though you value them but to actually value them for their own sakes. This is to say that Kant's deontology is fundamentally concerned with the internal attitude or motive of the truly moral agent, which he calls good will. Kant maintains that having a good will means doing your duty, which means universalizing your proposed actions because you regard others as ends in themselves.

Kant cautions that having good will in no way guarantees happiness. In fact, you may make yourself utterly miserable trying to be a moral person. But in trying to be a moral person you will at least be worthy of happiness, which is far more important, in his view, than actually being happy. If this approach to ethics is not your cup of tea, stay tuned for a diametrically opposed approach, coming to us via John Stuart Mill, in the next chapter.

Key ideas

A priori synthetic: The category of knowledge that does not depend on experience, even though it shapes that very experience
Categorical imperative: A universal moral requirement
Deontology: Ethical theory according to which rational beings discover the moral law within themselves in the form of duty
End in itself: Something that's worth having for its own sake
Good will: The internal attitude or motivation of the truly moral agent
Hypothetical imperative: An 'If ... then' statement that premises moral obligation upon a desired outcome
Maxim: A proposed course of action
Means to an end: Something that's worth having for the sake of something else
Noumenal realm: Things in themselves
Phenomenal realm: Things as they appear to the human mind
Transcendental idealism: The idea that the human mind does not experience ultimate reality but constructs a world of appearances

Fact-check

1 Kant's ethical theory is based on...
   a Finding happiness
   b Hypothetical imperatives
   c The Golden Rule
   d Good will

2 For which of the following reasons is Kant called a transcendental idealist?
   a He thinks the physical world is an illusion
   b He thinks ultimate reality is beyond human experience
   c He thinks all moral actions are universalizable
   d He thinks morality is relative to the culture you happen to belong to

3 Why can't rational agents disobey the categorical imperative, according to Kant?
   a It would be self-contradictory
   b It would make them unhappy
   c It would violate the Golden Rule
   d It would be too risky

4 Which of the following is an example of a categorical imperative?
   a Be generous
   b If you want to be successful, then you should be generous
   c Generosity is the mean between stinginess and prodigality
   d Never look a gift horse in the mouth

5 Which of the following statements reflects Kant's view of lying?
   a It's not wrong if you do it to protect someone else
   b It's wrong because it involves using people
   c It's not wrong if you do it to make someone happy
   d It's wrong because no one wants to live in a world full of liars

6 In which realm do things-in-themselves exist?
   a The noumenal
   b The phenomenal
   c The physical
   d The material

7 According to Kant, the problem with rationalism is which of the following?

   a It renders the mind a passive receptacle

   b It leaves us in doubt about the physical world

   c It implies that all values are relative to the culture to which you happen to belong

   d It is self-contradictory

8 What is the a priori synthetic?

   a A moral maxim derived from the categorical imperative

   b Another name for the phenomenal realm

   c A category of concepts that shape experience without depending on it

   d A hypothetical imperative that implies a self-contradiction

9 Which of the following is morally admirable, according to Kant?

   a Someone continues to work for social justice even though he doesn't really care any more

   b Someone allocates a portion of her income to charity every year to get a tax break

   c Someone writes a song for extra money, and the song makes a lot of people happy for many years to come

   d Someone knits her granddaughter a sweater to show she cares, but it turns out too small and prickly to wear

10 Which of the following are things-in-themselves, in Kant's view?

   a Actions that conform to the moral law

   b Physical objects

   c Time and space

   d Perfectly rational minds

Dig deeper

C. Korsgaard, *Creating the Kingdom of Ends* (Cambridge University Press, 1996).

A. Wood, *Kant* (Blackwell, 2005)

Virginia Heyer Young, *Ruth Benedict: Beyond Relativity, Beyond Pattern* (University of Nebraska Press, 2005)

Mill and happiness

'It is better to be a human being dissatisfied than a pig satisfied.'
John Stuart Mill

In this chapter you will learn:

▶ *about Mill's opposition to Kant*

▶ *why utilitarians think you should care about everyone's happiness*

▶ *how Bentham proposed to quantify pleasure*

▶ *why utilitarianism has led Singer to controversial views in applied ethics*

▶ *the significance of Mill's distinction between higher and lower pleasures*

▶ *the difference between act and rule utilitarianism*

▶ *about Mill's landmark defence of free speech.*

Thought experiment: runaway trolley

You've just started a new job at an amusement park supervising a ride that tours a reconstruction of New York City at the turn of the twentieth century. Riders learn some history and enjoy the old-world ambiance as they move up and down the realistic streets in trolley cars.

Your job is to sit in an observation booth on a bridge over the entrance to the ride and make sure everything goes smoothly. It's an easy job, insofar as the trolleys are almost completely automated, starting, stopping and turning in accordance with their programming. You have a control panel that tells you whether everything is in working order, along with a lever that enables you to switch the trolleys on to a sidetrack when they need maintenance.

For its finale, the trolley moves to the top of a hill and then slowly descends, giving its occupants a breathtaking view of New York Harbor. You have a great vantage point and like watching the people enjoying themselves. After you've been less than an hour on the job, however, disaster strikes.

A red light on your control panel starts blinking as a trolley climbs to the top of the final hill. The trolley's failsafe chain did not successfully engage. Fortunately, the failsafe chain is only needed in case the brakes fail. You'll simply switch the trolley to the sidetrack for maintenance.

As you watch the trolley begin its decent, however, a long low alarm begins to sound in your booth, signifying brake failure. You jump up in horror. The trolley is gaining momentum fast. Its five occupants begin screaming. They are heading straight towards a cement wall – with no seatbelts. Your control panel tells you that they are already approaching 100 km per hour (60 mph).

In a moment they will reach the split to the sidetrack, which makes a large circle into a maintenance area. If you switch the trolley to the sidetrack, it will miss the cement wall and slow down of its own accord.

You grip the lever. Just before you pull it, however, you catch sight of one of the maintenance workers kneeling on the sidetrack.

He seems to be tightening a bolt. He is completely unaware of the runaway trolley.

Your situation instantly crystallizes in your mind like frost on a freezing winter day. If you switch the trolley to the sidetrack, it will kill the maintenance man. If you don't make the switch, the inevitable crash will kill or seriously injure the five occupants of the trolley.

What should you do? What will you do?

Glancing back at the runaway trolley, you see a mother holding her infant child on board... Glancing back at the maintenance man, you suddenly recognize him as a good friend of yours...

Does any of this make a difference to your decision? Should it?

Do the right thing!

The runaway trolley thought experiment elaborated above is famous in philosophical circles for testing moral intuitions. As with the thought experiment at the opening of Chapter 1, people disagree widely about what to do and why. Many different versions have been invented, all with interesting implications.

The first point for us to note is that it's not clear what Kant's deontology would recommend. It all depends on exactly how we describe the situation. Suppose we formulate the following maxim:

'One should always strive to protect people from harm.'

Because you would fulfil this maxim five times over by saving the family on the runaway trolley, it seems you should switch the track. But suppose we formulate the following maxim instead:

'One should never deliberately harm someone.'

Because you would violate this maxim by causing the runaway trolley to hit the maintenance man, it seems you should not switch the track, allowing the family to crash into the cement wall.

Perhaps Kant's deontology can be interpreted in such a way as to yield a decisive answer in this situation. But perhaps not. And, if not, then it's inadequate, because ethical theories are supposed to be practical – guiding us in real-life moral dilemmas.

Utilitarianism

No one makes a better foil for Kant than the English philosopher John Stuart Mill (1806–73). While Kant was an eccentric recluse, Mill was an elected Member of Parliament. While Kant devoted his creative energy to working out the excruciating details of his transcendental vision, Mill lobbied for progressive political causes and was largely unconcerned about epistemological and metaphysical problems. While Kant regards happiness as incidental to morality, Mill regards it as morality's central aim.

Spotlight

Mill was educated at home by his demanding father. He began Classical Greek at age three and Latin at age seven. By the age of 12 he had learned the equivalent of a university degree. At the age of 20 he had a nervous breakdown. (Thanks, Dad.)

Mill's theory is called **utilitarianism**. Utilitarians maintain that, because happiness is the only worthy goal of human life, we must promote it whenever and wherever we can. The ethical act is the one that produces the greatest happiness for the greatest number of people.

Utilitarianism implies that you should switch the track and save the family because (presumably) more happiness is at stake for five people than for just one, even if he happens to be a good friend of yours. After all, each of the people on the trolley has good friends, too, who would be saddened by their deaths. As a utilitarian, your happiness counts just as much as, but no more than, anyone else's.

Unconcerned about the problems Kant and others saw in empiricism, Mill argued for utilitarianism based on experience.

It's not hard to show that each person desires his own happiness,
but why should I care about everyone else's happiness? Mill
would insist that, although it's sometimes difficult to see, our
own happiness is completely dependent on the happiness of
those around us.

Imagine that all your dreams have suddenly come true – you
are healthy, wealthy and wise. Although you are happier than
you ever thought possible, no one else is. Everyone at home, at
work, and in your neighbourhood is miserable. You walk down
the street humming merrily to yourself and see nothing but tears
and scowls everywhere you go. Could you remain happy in this
situation? Mill thinks not.

Hedonism

Mill did not invent utilitarianism. It was the brainchild of
his father's friend Jeremy Bentham (1748–1832), who was a
philosopher in his own right. Bentham advocated hedonism,
following the ancient Greek philosopher Epicurus (341–270 BC),
whose great advice to humankind was to eat, drink and be merry.

Bentham goes beyond Epicurus, however, in proposing a system,
known as the **hedonic calculus**, for quantifying pleasure. In
order to determine what action is right in a given situation, we

should use the following criteria to measure the pleasure that may come of it:

1 Intensity (How strong is the pleasure?)

2 Duration (How long is the pleasure likely to last?)

3 Certainty (How likely is the act to produce the expected pleasure?)

4 Propinquity (How soon is the act expected to produce the pleasure?)

5 Fecundity (Is this pleasure liable to produce more pleasure?)

6 Purity (Is this pleasure likely to be accompanied or followed by pain?)

7 Extent (How many people will experience the pleasure?)

Applying these criteria may yield surprising answers to moral dilemmas.

Suppose, for example, on a given afternoon, you have to choose between attending a friend's birthday party and helping your grandmother move to a retirement home. According to tradition, helping an aging relative is more important than partying. It's entirely possible, however, that the hedonic calculus would produce the opposite answer. If you and your friend really enjoy one another's company while you and your grandmother really don't, then you may be morally obligated to ignore tradition and have some fun.

Of course, following the hedonic calculus requires anticipating the future and estimating people's reactions, which can be a tricky business. Bentham and Mill agree, however, that such judgements are crucial for moral agency. Although no moral agent can hope to be entirely free from error in such judgements, we can all hope to improve through diligent observation.

Lazy Town

Mill sets happiness as the highest good and defines happiness specifically in terms of enjoying pleasure and avoiding pain.

Case study: Peter Singer and applied ethics

Towards the end of the twentieth century, philosophers carved out a new category of philosophy called **applied ethics**, which explores the implications of ethical theory for contemporary moral issues. Business ethics, environmental ethics and bioethics are three major areas of applied ethics.

Perhaps the most famous philosopher working in applied ethics today is the Australian Peter Singer (1956–). Singer has argued for a number of highly controversial utilitarian solutions to moral problems.

At the crux of Singer's interpretation of utilitarianism is the thesis that all and only beings with preferences are capable of experiencing pleasure and pain, and hence are worthy of ethical consideration. He draws the following conclusions:

▶ Because animals have preferences, meat-eating and all forms of factory farming are morally wrong.

▶ Because human foetuses are incapable of having preferences (at least through the first four and a half months of development), abortion is not morally wrong.

▶ Because people with various forms of brain damage (including Alzheimer's disease) have no preferences, euthanasia (mercy killing) is not morally wrong.

▶ Because human beings acquire preferences slowly as they gain rationality, autonomy and self-consciousness, killing a newborn infant is not as bad as killing a fully competent adult.

▶ Instances of bestiality, in which a human and an animal both voluntarily engage in sexual relations with one another, are not morally wrong.

▶ Since preferring luxuries is not as important as preferring basic needs, people in affluent nations are morally obligated to give their excess wealth to people in Third World nations.

Singer has written several bestselling books and appeared on popular television shows, including the American satirical news show *The Colbert Report*.

In so doing, he opens himself up to the objection that he is bound to create a base and repugnant society. After all, the art, literature, science and technology that make our civilization great took a lot of hard work. And hard work usually isn't so very pleasant.

Suppose every time he had the urge to write a symphony, Mozart simply opted to take a bubble bath instead. Writing a symphony involves a great deal of effort, with periods of frustration and even agony. Mill's theory seems to imply not only that Mozart is under no obligation to suffer for his music, but that he *shouldn't* suffer for it. Being morally obligated to maximize happiness, it seems he should do something more pleasant with his afternoon.

In fact, perhaps we should invent a pleasure machine that would stimulate the pleasure centre of the brain just like cocaine, except without the negative side effects. We could all plug in to the machine all day long and forget about ever accomplishing anything.

The concern for quality

Mill would point to two flaws in the above reasoning.

First, utilitarianism is not about maximizing pleasure for oneself only – it's about maximizing pleasure for *everyone*. So, if it turns out that Mozart can make a great deal of other people very happy with his music, then he is morally obligated to produce it after all. Far from being too lenient a theory, utilitarianism runs the risk of being too demanding, insofar as it requires us all to strive to maximize happiness for everyone all the time.

Second, unlike Bentham, Mill distinguishes between higher and lower pleasures. He would argue that playing music is more valuable than merely listening, and that writing music is more valuable than merely playing, even though the difficulty increases in each case.

Why is this?

Because the greater difficulty implies a greater satisfaction and value. In Mill's view, composing a symphony, despite the struggle involved in its creation, is so deeply satisfying and valuable that Mozart would never have traded it for an afternoon in the tub.

> It is indisputable that the being whose capacities of enjoyment are low, has the greatest chance of having them fully satisfied; and a highly endowed being will always feel that any happiness which he can look for, as the world is constituted, is imperfect. But he can learn to bear its imperfections, if they are at all bearable; and they will not make him envy the being who is indeed unconscious of the imperfections, but only because he feels not at all the good which those imperfections qualify. It is better to be a human being dissatisfied than a pig satisfied; better to be Socrates dissatisfied than a fool satisfied. And if the fool, or the pig, are a different opinion, it is because they only know their own side of the question. The other party to the comparison knows both sides.
>
> John Stuart Mill, *Utilitarianism*, Ch. 2 (http://www.utilitarianism.com/mill2htm)

We must all strive to become 'highly endowed beings' with a greater capacity for enjoyment of higher pleasures.

The greater satisfaction or value involved in higher pleasures is not captured by Bentham's hedonic calculus, which attempts to quantify pleasure in seven different ways. Mill's concern for higher pleasures adds, not an eighth way to quantify pleasure, but a whole new qualitative dimension. Mill's concern for the quality of pleasures takes his utilitarianism beyond Bentham's hedonism.

Of course, the question arises whether Mill can explain what exactly counts as a 'higher-quality pleasure' and why. What about those who like pop music better than Mozart? Do pop music lovers have a lower capacity for enjoyment? Or is the quality of a pleasure a completely subjective matter? Either possibility presents a challenge to someone who is trying to maximize happiness for everyone.

Acts vs. rules

Another common criticism of utilitarianism is that its relentless quest for happiness threatens to violate human rights. Consider the following scenario.

> You are the sheriff of a small town where a series of murders has occurred. You have good reason to believe the killer has skipped town, but an angry mob is convinced that the killer is a homeless man who wandered into town a week ago. The mob is preparing to riot unless you arrest and execute the homeless man. The homeless man has no family and would be easy to frame. The riot, on the other hand, would result in a great deal of property damage as well as injury and probably death. What should you do?

It looks as if a utilitarian will have to frame the homeless man. Yet most people intuitively feel that framing an innocent man is deeply wrong, regardless of the consequences of not doing so. We seem to have a sacred duty to uphold the truth and protect the innocent. How do we square this with the utilitarian directive to maximize happiness?

Mill suggests that, when we are considering whether an act is ethical, we shouldn't consider it alone as a one-time occurrence but rather as a type of action. This is to say that Mill promoted **rule utilitarianism** as opposed to **act utilitarianism**.

So, as sheriff, you shouldn't ask yourself which is more conducive to happiness: framing the homeless man or risking the riot? Instead, you should ask yourself which is more conducive to happiness: defending human rights or ignoring human rights? Overall, Mill thinks, you will find that cases like that of the sheriff are rare; for the most part, a society that recognizes rights is far happier than one that doesn't. By this reasoning, utilitarians must recognize rights.

Notice, however, that, even if you accept the rule-utilitarian approach, your conception of rights is not the same as the traditional conception. For example, the United States Declaration of Independence states: 'We hold these truths to be self-evident, that all men are created equal, that they are endowed by their Creator with certain unalienable Rights, that

among these are Life, Liberty and the pursuit of Happiness...'
For the utilitarian, a 'right' is nothing so noble – it's merely
shorthand for a policy that usually maximizes happiness.

Bentham, who was an act utilitarian, called rights 'nonsense
on stilts'. Needless to say, he was critical of the Declaration of
Independence and the entire American Revolution.

Liberty and equality

While Bentham's hedonistic utilitarianism made him politically
conservative, Mill's qualitative, rule utilitarianism made him a
progressive. He wrote a book called *The Subjection of Women*
(1869) in which he makes a pioneering argument for female
suffrage (women's right to vote). He campaigned for this reform
on utilitarian grounds in Parliament in 1865. Being ahead of his
time, he was of course roundly defeated, but he put the issue on
the table so forcefully that it never went away.

Spotlight

Harriet Taylor (1807–58) was Mill's great collaborator in life.
Although she was married to another man and already the mother
of three when she met Mill, she immediately began exchanging
ideas with him and reading his work. Without divorcing, she
separated from her husband so that she could pursue a platonic
(yeah, right) relationship with Mill. After 21 years and the death
of Taylor's husband, the two philosophers finally married. Mill
credits Taylor as a co-author for most of his publications. He was
heartbroken when she died just seven years later.

Mill also wrote a book called *On Liberty*, which advanced the
cause of political liberalism launched by his predecessor John
Locke, whom we met in Chapter 7. Mill uses his utilitarian
principles to argue for greater freedom and equality. Beyond
exhorting the reader to choose government policies that
will maximize happiness, he points to the positive long-term
consequences of liberalism. Utilitarianism is sometimes called
consequentialism because it is concerned not with principles but
with results.

For example, Mill makes an impassioned case for free speech. Someone might be in favour of censorship based on a duty to uphold and defend the truth. Mill argues, however, that such a policy has disastrous consequences for four main reasons.

1 The censored opinion may turn out to be true.

2 It may contain a portion of the truth or an error that helps bring the truth to light.

3 Even if the censored opinion is completely false, letting it air will prompt a vigorous defence of the truth, which keeps it from becoming an empty prejudice.

4 People develop character through the experience of defending the truth.

At the heart of Mill's liberalism is the conviction that the freedom and equality promoted by political liberalism are required in order for human beings to develop individuality, and individuality is crucial for becoming a 'highly endowed being' capable of enjoying the higher-quality pleasures that constitute true happiness.

It really is of importance, not only what men do, but also what manner of men they are that do it. Among the works of man, which human life is rightly employed in perfecting and beautifying, the first in importance surely is man himself. Supposing it were possible to get houses built, corn grown, battles fought, causes tried, and even churches erected and prayers said, by machinery – by automatons in human form – it would be a considerable loss to exchange for these automatons even the men and women who at present inhabit the more civilized parts of the world, and who assuredly are but starved specimens of what nature can and will produce. Human nature is not a machine to be built after a model, and set to do exactly the work prescribed for it, but a tree, which requires to grow and develop itself on all sides, according to the tendency of the inward forces which make it a living thing.

John Stuart Mill, *On Liberty*, Ch. 3 (http://www.bartleby.com/130/3html)

While being concerned only with results, Mill at the same time insists that it matters how the results are achieved. This is an interesting tension in his position. Critics regard it as a condemning contradiction; supporters regard it as an opportunity for further development.

Spotlight

Bentham left instructions for his body to be embalmed, dressed and placed sitting in a display case at University College, the university for nonconformists that he helped to found in London. Because his head became horrifically misshapen during the embalming process, it was replaced with a wax likeness. Bentham's body remains on display today, cheerfully greeting passers-by. On the 100th and 150th anniversaries of the university it was brought to the university council meeting and listed as 'present, but not voting'.

Key ideas

Act utilitarianism: The view that, when considering whether an act is ethical, we should consider it alone as a one-time occurrence
Applied ethics: The area of philosophy that explores the implications of ethical theories for contemporary moral issues
Consequentialism: Another name for utilitarianism because it is concerned not with principles but with results
Hedonic calculus: Bentham's system for quantifying pleasure
Hedonism: An ethical theory that recommends maximizing pleasure and avoiding pain, with attention to the quantity not the quality of the pleasure
Rule utilitarianism: When considering whether an act is ethical, we should consider it as a type of action rather than a one-time occurrence
Utilitarianism: The view that the ethical act is the one that produces the greatest happiness for the greatest number of people, where happiness is conceived in terms of higher-quality pleasures

Fact-check

1 On which of the following grounds might a utilitarian argue against lying?
  a Lying is a sin against God
  b Lying tends to make people unhappy
  c When rational agents lie they contradict themselves
  d Truly rational agents cannot lie

2 What is the difference between hedonism and utilitarianism?
  a Hedonists are concerned about the quality of the pleasure; utilitarians are not
  b Utilitarians are concerned about the quality of the pleasure; hedonists are not
  c Hedonists consider the ethical act as a type of action; utilitarians consider it as a one-time occurrence
  d Utilitarians consider the ethical act as a type of action; hedonists consider it as a one-time occurrence

3 Which of the following authors was against the American Revolution?
  a Bentham
  b Mill
  c Kant
  d Singer

4 Singer is against meat-eating on which of the following grounds?
  a It's unhealthy
  b It's an unnecessary luxury
  c Animals are unclean
  d Animals prefer to live a pleasant life

5 Which of the following is a rule-utilitarian consideration?
  a If I cheat on this test, I might get caught
  b Cheating violates the duty to be honest
  c Truly rational agents are incapable of cheating
  d Cheating tends to cause more problems than it solves

6 Which of the following is *not* one of the criteria in Bentham's hedonic calculus?
  a Intensity
  b Propinquity
  c Extent
  d Quality

7 Which of the following is a question from applied ethics?
  a Should I tell my children the truth about Santa Claus?
  b Is it wrong for businesses to produce toxic waste?
  c Why should I be moral?
  d Does moral obligation come from reason or experience?

8 Mill and Bentham were both which of the following?
  a Political liberals
  b Rationalists
  c Empiricists
  d Hedonists

9 Which of the following is *not* one of Mill's arguments for free speech?
  a Everyone has a natural right to speak their mind
  b False opinions may help bring the truth to light
  c Censored opinions may turn out to be true
  d Defending the truth gives people character

10 Why do people need freedom and equality, according to Mill?
  a To develop individuality
  b To earn a better income
  c To uphold traditional duties
  d To avoid hard work

Dig deeper

Thomas Nagel, *The Possibility of Altruism*, new edn (Princeton University Press, 2012)

H.O. Pappe, *John Stuart Mill and Harriet Taylor* (University of Melbourne Press, 1960)

J. Skorupski, *John Stuart Mill* (Routledge, 1989)

11

Nietzsche and meaning

'When you look into an abyss, the abyss also looks into you.'
Friedrich Nietzsche

In this chapter you will learn:

▶ *why Nietzsche despises all modern religion*
▶ *about the will to power, Nietzsche's most famous thesis*
▶ *the meaning of Zarathustra's announcement that God is dead*
▶ *about the godlike being whom Nietzsche called the Übermensch*
▶ *the significance of the Greek gods Apollo and Dionysus for Nietzsche's philosophy*
▶ *about nihilism and its relation to perspectivalism*
▶ *How Heidegger investigated 'the being' of being itself*
▶ *the meaning of continental philosophy.*

Thought experiment: eternal recurrence

You wake up in the morning to your phone ringing.

'Hello?' you sputter.

It's your boss. Today is your birthday and, although you were scheduled to work a long shift, your boss has found a way to give you the day off instead.

'Take it free and clear, as a gift.'

'But...'

'No "buts!"' your boss chimes merrily. 'Everything is taken care of. Only one thing is required of you.' Here, your boss's voice turns serious. 'Make the most of this day. I mean really seize it. You must live this day like it was the last day of your life.'

You hang up the phone, suspicious. Have you been exposed to some fatal radiation that will kill you by midnight?

'Suppose that were true... How would I spend this day?' you wonder.

A few ideas occur to you: max your credit cards out with a flight to Paris or Napa Valley and dinner in the most expensive restaurant you can find...

But who wants to spend their last day on a plane, and, besides, who will end up paying the debt? It doesn't seem fair to leave that behind...

Better to spend the day in the company of friends, you decide, and set about calling people. But, of course, everyone is busy with work and school, the never-ending demands of their lives. No one is available to play hooky with you.

'Well, there are a few things I've been meaning to get done... Starting with a good shave, a few errands, then maybe some shopping. After I take care of some things, I can sit down and think about what I might like to do with my day...'

The day goes by quickly.

It was a good day. You got a bunch of things done and didn't have to hurry up to go anywhere. But it wasn't an especially great day – on the boring side, actually. You finally sit down with a tub of ice cream wondering once again whether you will be dead by midnight.

'Is there anything I should do tonight, just in case?'

But thinking about it makes you tired and before long you are in a deep sleep...

You wake up in the morning to your phone ringing.

'Hello?' you sputter.

It's your boss. Today is your birthday and, although you were scheduled to work a long shift, your boss has found a way to give you the day off instead.

'Take it free and clear, as a gift.'

'But...'

'No "buts!"' your boss chimes merrily. 'Everything is taken care of. Only one thing is required of you.' Here, your boss's voice turns serious. 'Make the most of this day. I mean really seize it. You must live this day like it was the last day of your life.'

You hang up the phone, suspicious. Have you been exposed to some fatal radiation that will kill you by midnight?

'Suppose that were true... How would I spend this day?' ... ...

You better love your life

'I love my life!' Can you honestly say that? How many people do you think can?

When pressed, most people will admit that, although they do not absolutely love their life right now, they fully intend to love it just as soon as _____. Fill this blank with something like one of the following:

▶ 'just as soon as I finish school'

▶ 'just as soon as I find a better job'

▶ 'just as soon as I meet the right person'

- ▶ 'just as soon as I can afford a house'

- ▶ 'just as soon as I have a family of my own'

- ▶ 'just as soon as my children are older'

- ▶ 'just as soon as I lose some weight'

- ▶ 'just as soon as my divorce is final'

and so on…

When you're young, you're completely convinced by the illusion of a light at the end of the tunnel. Somewhere in middle age, however, it will dawn on you that every 'just as soon as' is replaced by another, and that there really is no end to them in this life. This thought often inspires people to believe fervently in an afterlife where somehow, finally, you get a life that you can really love.

The thought experiment at the opening of this chapter, where you find yourself living the same day over again, was originally proposed by the German philosopher Friedrich Nietzsche (1844–1900). Nietzsche viewed the 'just as soon as' mentality as the most significant problem of Western civilization. He asks us to suppose we are condemned to repeat our lives the same way over and over again for ever – an eternal recurrence. This should inspire you to do whatever it takes to be sure you love every moment.

The will to power

Nietzsche was a bold and daring cultural critic. The son of a Lutheran pastor, he launched his career with a scathing criticism of Christianity. Christianity invented the 'just as soon as' mentality discussed above by teaching that this life is just a transitory struggle on the way to heaven. But Christianity invented and perpetuates many other problematic attitudes as well, in his view.

In particular, the chief virtues according to Christianity, as demonstrated by its messiah, Jesus Christ, are humility and sacrifice. But these are slavish qualities, worthy only of servile, inferior beings, according to Nietzsche.

People tend to think of morality as something so sacred that it cannot be questioned. But Nietzsche argues that, if you trace the emergence of moral concepts through Western civilization, you'll see that they are just human constructs, born of the ongoing struggle between individuals and groups for the only thing that really matters – power.

When Nietzsche examines reality to see what it is truly made of, he finds nothing but power. All of nature – everything that exists – is striving to impose itself on the world. Every rock, tree, bird and bee wants to spread itself out, to dominate its environment. Human beings are no different, and exerting ourselves always means confronting and overcoming others. Whether we acknowledge it or not, we are all pushing to seize the highest possible position in life – an instinctual urge Nietzsche calls the 'will to power'.

Nietzsche asks: are you going to try to suppress this urge, or are you going to make the most of it?

Master–slave morality

The history of morality is the history of a power struggle between masters – the strong ones who have succeeded in imposing their will – and slaves – the weak ones who have been imposed upon. Christians started out as slaves but slowly turned the tables on their masters by cloaking their ambition in the language of love.

Nietzsche despises Christianity, Judaism and, by extension, all modern religions, for their covert and hypocritical agenda. He writes: 'After coming into contact with a religious man I always feel I must wash my hands.'

Nietzsche instead admires the master morality – which he calls 'noble' and identifies with prehistoric man – because at least it is honest and courageous. The masters rape, pillage and plunder without apology, creating their own value along the way.

While Nietzsche has no qualms about bashing traditional morality and religion, there is a method in his madness. He is determined to help his readers break free of the sour malaise in which he feels modern society is drowning.

Zarathustra

Perhaps because his ideas were so controversial, or perhaps because his own way of thinking was so unconventional, Nietzsche conveyed much of his philosophy through fiction. His most important character, Zarathustra, is based on the Iranian prophet by the same name (also known as Zoroaster).

Zarathustra, who is clearly a projection of Nietzsche himself, left his home to seek wisdom in the mountains. After ten years, he returned to society to share with the people the shocking truth he learned: that 'God is dead'.

In asserting that God is dead, Nietzsche does not mean to be taken literally – that God was once alive. On the contrary, God never existed, in Nietzsche's view; he was always just a story the masters told to keep the slaves from rebelling. But there was a time when the story of God enlivened the people, inspiring them to achieve great things. And this is what has died. The story doesn't work any more. It's just a tired old tale that creates timid, uninteresting people who do nothing but 'follow the herd' like sheep.

Through the figure of Zarathustra, Nietzsche argues, not that we adopt the master morality, but that we transcend the master–slave dichotomy altogether. He implores us to evolve 'beyond good and evil'.

Spotlight

Seen on a washroom wall:

God is dead. – Nietzsche

Nietzsche is dead. – God

Übermensch

Just as ape-like creatures evolved into humanity, humanity is capable of evolving into a more advanced form of existence – godlike beings, whom Nietzsche calls the *Übermenschen*. The **Übermensch** (named from a German word that roughly translates as 'over-man') is the ultimate realization of the will to power. He is neither slave nor master, because he is completely self-sufficient.

Since no one has yet achieved this level of existence, we can't be sure exactly what it would be like. Nevertheless, Nietzsche suggests that the pagan culture of ancient Greece provides a good clue.

The ancient Greeks developed their religious and moral concepts through tragedy – dramatic performances about human suffering that were regularly staged for the public. According to Nietzsche's analysis, the best tragedies always revolved around two opposed forces: the **Apollonian** and the **Dionysian**.

Named after Apollo, the sun god, the Apollonian force is rational and law-like. It seeks to preserve and protect by maintaining strict order. The Dionysian force, in contrast, named after Dionysus, the god of wine, is dangerous, cruel and wild. It seeks to unleash chaos at every turn. Greek tragedy shows how both forces have an important role to play and are required for a balanced, healthy existence.

Problems began for Western civilization when Socrates, whom Nietzsche regards as a menace rather than a hero, promoted the Apollonian force over the Dionysian force. This rationalistic trend was reinforced by Christianity, which strove to tame and deny all ecstatic instincts. The result is a highly repressed society. The solution, and the path to humanity's next evolution, is to reintroduce the Dionysian force, both on an individual and a societal level.

The divine ecstasy of the Übermensch must be distinguished from the utilitarian happiness of John Stuart Mill, whom Nietzsche called 'the flathead'. 'Man does not strive for happiness,' Nietzsche writes, 'only the Englishman does that.' Mill seeks to maximize pleasure and minimize pain – a trivial and unworthy aspiration from Nietzsche's perspective. The Übermensch, in contrast, lives deeply, richly and significantly without shying away from pain, because, as Nietzsche famously remarks, 'that which does not kill us makes us stronger'. The Übermensch is an uncontainable force of nature, who rejects all value systems while living life to the hilt.

Nihilism/perspectivalism

Nietzsche openly identified himself as a **nihilist** (from the Latin word for 'nothing'). By this, he means that there is no objective meaning in the world. Every belief is false because there is no true reason for anything.

But without God, the universe is meaningless. Life is meaningless. We're meaningless. [Long pause] I have a sudden and overpowering urge to get laid.

Woody Allen

Needless to say, nihilism is a rare position to find among philosophers. Why write books, why even get up in the morning, if there is no point to anything? Yet Nietzsche did get up in the morning and continued to write books even through a debilitating illness that caused a mental breakdown leading to his early death at age 55. How did he make sense of the meaninglessness he felt he had discovered?

Once again casting his gaze over the history of Western civilization, Nietzsche observes that nihilism is the logical conclusion of all of its striving. He predicts that, just as individuals eventually realize their 'just as soon as' mentality to be futile, so, too, society itself will realize that all its goals are illusory.

> *Nihilism as a psychological state will have to be reached, first, when we have sought a 'meaning' in all events that is not there: so the seeker eventually becomes discouraged. Nihilism, then, is the recognition of the long waste of strength, the agony of the 'in vain', insecurity, the lack of any opportunity to recover and to regain composure – being ashamed in front of oneself, as if one had deceived oneself all too long. This meaning could have been: the 'fulfilment' of some highest ethical canon in all events, the moral world order; or the growth of love and harmony in the intercourse of beings; or the gradual approximation of a state of universal happiness; or even the development towards a state of universal annihilation – any goal at least constitutes some meaning. What all these notions have in common is that something is to be achieved through the process – and now one realizes that becoming aims at nothing and achieves nothing.*
> Friedrich Nietzsche, *The Will to Power*, Book 1 (http://www.yuga.com/ Cgi/Pag.dll?Pag=107)

One goal leads to another and another in an aimless series rather than progressive improvement. All of our apparent achievements (one thinks, for instance, of the latest mobile phone) are really just superficial distractions from a hollow lack of substance at the centre.

While it may be upsetting to come to this realization, it is also liberating. It forces one to realize that one is free to make one's own meaning. Rather than giving up in the face of nothingness, Nietzsche transforms his nihilism into perspectivalism, arguing that, while there is no absolute truth, everyone can develop their own interpretation of the world. His emphasis on the radical freedom of interpretation has made him an important influence on the art world.

Case study: Heidegger and phenomenology

The twentieth-century German philosopher Martin Heidegger (1889–1976) was profoundly influenced by Nietzsche. He argues that the history of Western philosophy was bound to produce a nihilist because it set off on the wrong foot from the very beginning.

Philosophers have always been engaged in metaphysical investigations, asking about the nature of reality. As we have seen in this book: Plato asks whether the material world exists; Aquinas and Anselm ask whether God exists; Descartes asks whether the soul exists; Hobbes asks whether freedom exists; Hume asks whether causality exists; and so on, up to Nietzsche, who concluded that nothing but the will to power exists. Philosophers are always asking whether things that seem to exist really do exist and, if so, whether it can be proven.

The problem, according to Heidegger, is that they all take it for granted that we understand what existence is. They fail to ask what it means for something to be real in the first place. This is the fundamental question that must be answered before any others can even be asked. What is it to be? We cannot investigate the being of particular beings until we investigate the being of being itself.

So Heidegger sets out to investigate the being of being – a very esoteric enterprise! In fact, the very idea of the 'being of being' is so odd that it is scarcely intelligible. Yet Heidegger writes that 'Making itself intelligible is suicide for philosophy', and his magnum opus, *Being and Time* (1927), has been called the most influential single philosophical work of the twentieth century.

The method of Heidegger's investigation is called **hermeneutical phenomenology**. Phenomenology refers to the study of the structure of consciousness. Like his teacher Edmund Husserl, who was the founder of phenomenology, Heidegger believes that subjective experience gives us the greatest clue to the truth about reality.

For example, we cannot understand a hammer by looking at it as a separate object but only by using it and thereby, in a way, merging our being with its being. The attempt to maintain a subject–object distinction leads to many of the misunderstandings that have corrupted the history of philosophy.

Rather than rejecting this history, however, Heidegger believes we must reinterpret it. This is why his phenomenology is hermeneutic: by studying historical texts and thinking about their traditional conceptions of the world in new ways we gain valuable insights.

The main insight Heidegger hits upon in *Being and Time* is the concept of **Dasein**, which means 'being there' and refers to the experience of being that is peculiar to humanity. It is a form of consciousness that must deal with such issues as personhood, caring about things, the passage of time, and death.

Despite the enthusiastic reception of *Being and Time*, Heidegger claimed his effort to discover the meaning of being to be a failure, and he never finished his planned sequel to the book. To make matters worse, in later years he seems to take back, or at least modify, much of what he originally wrote.

Of course, it's not all unusual for anyone, much less philosophers, to revise their point of view over the course of a lifetime. Nevertheless, Heidegger may win the prize for being the most impossible-to-understand philosopher of all time.

Spotlight

Although his teacher Edmund Husserl and his lover Hannah Arendt were Jews, Heidegger became a member of the Nazi party and never, to his dying day in 1976, expressed regret about it.

Continental philosophy

Nietzsche, Husserl and Heidegger, along with Sartre, whom we will meet in Chapter 13, are considered the founders of **continental philosophy**. The term 'continental philosophy' was coined in the last quarter of the twentieth century to distinguish thought stemming from the continent of Europe from analytic philosophy, which is characteristic of Great Britain.

While continental philosophy includes a variety of original thinkers, the following themes dominate among them:

▶ a preference for literary and poetic forms of expression over ordinary language

▶ the rejection of a single, objective or scientific point of view

▶ the effort to situate concepts within their cultural, historical or political context

▶ an emphasis on the freedom of the individual

▶ concern with the methods and aims of philosophy as a discipline.

Continental philosophy is best understood in contrast to analytic philosophy, and so we turn to it next.

Key ideas

Analytic philosophy: Thought characteristic of Great Britain
Apollonian force: The rational and orderly theme in Greek tragedy
Continental philosophy: Thought characteristic of the continent of Europe
Dionysian force: The dangerous, cruel and wild theme in Greek tragedy
Eternal recurrence: How would you live your life if you knew you had to repeat it the same way over and over again for ever?
Dasein: The experience of being that is peculiar to humanity
Hermeneutics: The reinterpretation of historical texts and traditional concepts
Nihilism: The view that there is no objective meaning in the world
Perspectivalism: The view that, while there is no absolute truth, everyone can develop their own interpretation of the world
Phenomenology: The study of the structure of consciousness
Übermensch: The 'over-man' – the godlike existence towards which human beings are capable of evolving
Will to power: The instinctual urge to seize the highest possible position in life

Fact-check

1 When Nietzsche asserted that 'God is dead', he meant which of the following?
  a That God is actually alive
  b That the story of God no longer inspires great things
  c That people have lost their religious faith
  d That the being of God is unintelligible

2 Which of the following authors was the founder of phenomenology?
  a Nietzsche
  b Husserl
  c Heidegger
  d Sartre

3 Nietzsche ultimately advocates which of the following?
  a The master morality
  b The slave morality
  c Utilitarianism
  d None of the above

4 Which of the following questions concerned Heidegger?
  a What would the Übermensch be like?
  b How can we maximize happiness and minimize pain?
  c How did Christianity corrupt Western civilization?
  d What is the meaning of being?

5 Which of the following leads Nietzsche to nihilism?
  a Worshipping an unintelligible God
  b Seeking meaning only to discover that there is none
  c Making the most of the will to power
  d Raping, pillaging and plundering without apology

6 What does Nietzsche intend to accomplish through the eternal recurrence?
  a To discover the meaning of being itself
  b To spread out and dominate his environment
  c To inspire his readers to love their life
  d To take back much of what he originally wrote

7 Which of the following would Nietzsche admire the most?
   a Alexander the Great
   b St Thomas Aquinas
   c Plato
   d Peter Singer

8 Which of the following is Nietzsche's most likely pick for a great way to spend a day off from writing?
   a Bow-and-arrow hunting
   b Helping the poor
   c Touring a medieval cathedral
   d Playing chess

9 Which of the following is *not* a dominant theme among continental philosophers?
   a The use of clear and ordinary language
   b The rejection of a single, objective or scientific point of view
   c An emphasis on the freedom of the individual
   d Concern with the methods and aims of philosophy as a discipline

10 Why has Nietzsche's perspectivalism influenced the art world?
   a Because it argues that there is no point to anything
   b Because it emphasizes the radical freedom of interpretation
   c Because it revitalized interest in Greek tragedy
   d Because it shows how studying historical texts and their traditional ideas of the world yields valuable insights

Dig deeper

Lawrence J. Hatab, *Nietzsche's Life Sentence: Coming to Terms with Eternal Recurrence* (Routledge, 2005)

S. Mulhall, *Routledge Philosophy Guidebook to Heidegger and 'Being and Time'*, second edn (Routledge, 2005)

Bernard Reginster, *The Affirmation of Life: Nietzsche on Overcoming Nihilism* (Harvard University Press, 2006)

12

Wittgenstein and language

'If a lion could talk, we could not understand him.'
Ludwig Wittgenstein

In this chapter you will learn:

▶ *why Wittgenstein rejected metaphysics*

▶ *the import of the picture theory of meaning*

▶ *about Wittgenstein's contribution to formal logic*

▶ *the role of logic in analytic philosophy*

▶ *why language is a game according to the later Wittgenstein*

▶ *the philosophical significance of family resemblance*

▶ *why Wittgenstein denied that minds exist*

▶ *about Wittgenstein's connection to behaviourism.*

Thought experiment: iMe

The doorbell rings. You peer out of the window. Standing on the steps are two men in suits, one with dark hair, the other blond. The one with dark hair notices you at the window and flashes a badge.

It says FBI.

Nervous, but also curious, you open the door. The dark-haired officer introduces himself and his partner and asks to speak with you inside.

'We won't take much of your time.'

You let them in.

After some small talk and basic questions about your life and work, to which they already seem to know the answers, the officer with dark hair gets down to business.

'We're here to ask you about your co-workers. How many of your co-workers would you classify as androids?'

You raise your eyebrows. 'You mean robots?'

Your interviewer is nodding.

'Wow,' you reply, surprised by the line of questioning. 'I mean, we have a lot of computers, of course... But I haven't seen anything more advanced than that.'

The officers glance at one another, stone-faced.

'Do any of your co-workers behave in a way you consider... odd?'

A moment of silence passes while you think about what he is asking.

'Well, they're all a little odd, I suppose. Aren't we all?'

'Sure,' he agrees. 'But there's odd and then there's... not quite human.'

You feel your brows knitting your forehead tightly together. The faces of your co-workers are flipping rapidly through your mind. Are some of them robots? Is it really possible to make robots that realistic now? You look from one officer to the other for a sign that this interview is some kind of joke.

It's then that you notice something off about the blond officer. He seems to be wearing a wig. And his skin is shiny, a little too shiny. His eyes are occluded behind tinted glasses.

You freeze in your seat, realizing that he hasn't spoken yet.

'I'm sorry, what was your name again?' you force yourself to ask the blond officer.

'Agent Tom Blandish,' he replies. And his voice is not quite right. Not quite right at all. You feel your skin crawling under your clothes and an overwhelming urge to get away – fast.

'I'm sorry I couldn't help you, officers,' you stammer, rising to your feet, 'but I'm... late for an appointment... and so I need to ask you to leave now.'

The officers stand. The dark-haired one tilts his head, squinting at the back of your neck.

'It's in the back,' he tells his partner. 'Go ahead and press it now.'

Your hand flies to the back of your neck to see whether you can feel what he's referring to. A shiver of panic rushes through your body. You begin backing towards the door.

Before you can get away, Agent Blandish grabs your arm with superhuman strength and reaches around your neck. Before you can make another move, you hear the 'click' of a button and the lights go out.

Organic machines

No doubt you would be shocked to learn you were an android. You probably feel quite certain you're not. After reading the above thought experiment, you weren't overwhelmed with the need to feel for a button at the back of your neck.

And yet, human beings are machines – organic machines – meaning that we grew naturally rather than being made artificially. Few people would contest the claim that our bodies are machines; the claim many would contest is that this is *all* we are.

What is it that's so disturbing about the idea of talking to, working with or being an android? Engineers are creating more and more realistic androids every year. If one of them was standing before you right now, would you find it creepy? Would you have a sense that no one's 'home'?

How do you know anyone is ever 'home'? All the cues (focused eyes, facial expression, tone of voice, tiny movements, a subtle scent, radiating warmth, etc.) can, in theory, be reproduced artificially. If we can make androids that behave exactly like human beings, do we have any right to believe that there is something more to us? Not at all, according to the Austrian philosopher Ludwig Wittgenstein (1889–1951). Wittgenstein's analysis of human language eventually led him to the thesis that no one is ever really 'home'.

The mystery of language

Though he was from continental Europe, Wittgenstein studied in England with the great logician Bertrand Russell (1872–1970) because he wasn't interested in the poetic metaphysics of continental philosophy. His first undertaking was to develop an account of language according to which all traditional metaphysics (such as idealism, which we examined in Chapter 2, or Descartes's dualism, which we examined in Chapter 5) is literally nonsense. It begins with a careful analysis of reference – the way words connect to the world.

How is it that we refer to things when we speak?

Suppose you and I meet by chance out in the street, and you say, 'Where's your dog?' The sounds you make (represented here with marks on a page) cause me to think about what you were thinking about. Your words are very powerful: they somehow point to a particular object, drawing my attention to that object, even against my will. How can mere sounds (and marks) wield such power? This is actually a great mystery, though we take it for granted every day.

Wittgenstein's first attempt at a solution is known as the 'picture theory of meaning'. It holds that words correspond to the world in the same way pictures do. Suppose that, when you ask me where my dog is, I respond: 'He's sleeping in my kitchen.' I've presented a picture of my dog sleeping in my kitchen. If this corresponds to the actual 'state of affairs' in the world, then the sentence is true; if it doesn't, then the sentence is false.

Notice that you can't make a picture of something unless it's physically observable. Metaphysics, by definition, goes beyond the physical world. It tries to refer to things like God, the soul, free will, causality, conscience, and so on, none of which can be observed. It therefore goes beyond the reach of human language on Wittgenstein's account. No wonder, then, that traditional metaphysics is so hard to understand: it's literally unintelligible!

Logic

Wittgenstein asserts that any intelligible statement, called a 'proposition', has **truth value**, meaning that it is either true or false. He developed a method for assigning truth value to complex propositions from their atomic parts. Known as 'truth tables', this method has become a standard component of formal logic.

Formal logic is the systematic study of the relationship between propositions. Logicians use variables, such as 'P' and 'Q', to represent propositions and symbols such as '¬' and '∧' to represent operations, or ways propositions are used.

Consider the following two propositions:

P: The dog is sleeping in the kitchen.

Q: It is raining.

I can use these two sentences in a variety of ways. For example, I can say, 'The dog is not sleeping in the kitchen.' This negation would be symbolized as:

¬P

Or I can say 'The dog is sleeping in the kitchen and it is raining.' This conjunction would be symbolized as:

P ∧ Q

Needless to say, propositions can become very complicated. The logician's job is to break them down into their atomic parts and show what they imply, without making any assumptions about whether they are true or false. Wittgenstein's truth tables help with this process by assigning all the possible truth values in a simple format.

For example, the truth table for the conjunction P ^ Q looks like this:

	P	Q	P^Q
1	True	True	True
2	True	False	False
3	False	True	False
4	False	False	False

This table shows that the logical operator conjunction can operate on P and Q in four different ways.

▶ The first line shows that when P and Q are both true, then the conjunction is true.

▶ The second line shows that when P is true and Q is false, then the conjunction is false.

▶ The third line shows that when P is false and Q is true, then the conjunction is false.

▶ The fourth line shows that when P and Q are both false, then the conjunction is false.

Bearing in mind that P and Q can stand for any propositions, the truth table proves that any conjunction is true only when both propositions are true, and false otherwise.

Granted, this is not an earth-shattering revelation! Any three-year-old who can put sentences together with the word 'and' already knows what this truth table proves. But we've looked at only one very simple example. The same process can be used to analyse extremely complex sets of propositions. Formal logic is very useful in clarifying human language, as any computer programmer knows.

Case study: Bertrand Russell and strange genius

Wittgenstein's teacher, Bertrand Russell, launched his career with a massive three-volume work called *Principia Mathematica* in which he and his co-author, Alfred North Whitehead, set out to prove that 1 + 1 = 2. They were not successful.

You thought that was an easy one, huh? Then give it a try yourself.

Hint: you may need to come up with a complete set of axioms and inference rules for all of mathematics.

On second thoughts, don't bother trying. After reading *Principia Mathematica*, the Austrian-American logician Kurt Gödel proved that the complete set it requires is impossible because, for any set of axioms and inference rules, there will always be some truths of mathematics that cannot be deduced from it.

Oh well. So much can be learned from an epic failure.

Russell went on to write on a wide range of philosophical subjects, most of which were much more accessible than the *Principia Mathematica*. In fact, he received the Nobel Prize in Literature for championing humanitarian ideals and freedom of thought.

No ordinary chump himself, Russell gives us insight into Wittgenstein's strange genius. He writes:

> *I got a letter from Wittgenstein written from Monte Cassino, saying that a few days after the Armistice, he had been taken prisoner by the Italians, but fortunately with his manuscript. It appears he had written a book in the trenches, and wished me to read it. He was the kind of man who would never have noticed such small matters as bursting shells when he was thinking about logic. [...] It was the book which was subsequently published under the title* Tractatus. *[...] Just about at the time of the Armistice his father had died, and Wittgenstein inherited the bulk of his fortune. He came to the conclusion, however, that money is a nuisance to a philosopher, so he gave every penny of it to his brother and sisters. Consequently he was unable to pay the fare from Vienna to The Hague, and was far too proud to accept it from me. [...] He must have suffered during this time hunger and considerable privation, though it was very seldom that he could be induced to say anything about it, as he had the pride of Lucifer. At last his sister decided to build a house, and employed him as an architect. This gave him enough to eat for several years...*

> The Autobiography of Bertrand Russell (London: Routledge, 2010 [1968]), pp. 330–31)

In truth, philosophers have always been known for their eccentricities.

Analytic philosophy

In his quest for precision, Wittgenstein went beyond logic, helping to found the analytic school of philosophy.

Many philosophers, especially in England and the United States, continue to follow Wittgenstein's lead in using logic to break down and analyse lofty philosophical claims, banishing nonsense whenever they can.

The object of philosophy is the logical clarification of thoughts.

Philosophy is not a theory but an activity. A philosophical work consists essentially of elucidations. The result of philosophy is not a number of 'philosophical propositions', but to make propositions clear.

Philosophy should make clear and delimit sharply the thoughts which otherwise are, as it were, opaque and blurred.
Ludwig Wittgenstein, *Tractatus Logico-Philosophicus* 4.112 (http://www.gutenberg.org/files/5740/5740-pdf.pdf)

The above passage comes from the *Tractatus*, in which Wittgenstein developed his truth tables and his picture theory of meaning. This work defines the early part of Wittgenstein's career. Having dismissed metaphysics and apparently solved the mystery of language, Wittgenstein pursued architecture, thinking there was no work left to be done in philosophy.

But he was dragged back. According to legend, someone who had read the *Tractatus*, and disagreed with it, crudely gave Wittgenstein the finger, saying 'Picture this!' Astonished, Wittgenstein instantly abandoned his picture theory of meaning. He evidently realized that making a crude gesture is a paradigm instance of human language, and it isn't like making a picture – it's more like making a move in a game.

The builder's game

The later Wittgenstein developed a theory of language that doesn't rely on reference at all.

Suppose you're observing two men building a house. 'Builder A' calls out 'Slab!' 'Builder B' goes to the pile of slabs, picks one up and brings it to Builder A. Then Builder A calls out 'Beam!', and Builder B brings him a beam. Builder A goes on calling out words – slab, block, pillar and beam. In each case, Builder B retrieves the correct object.

At first glance, we might think their communication works as follows: Builder has a thought in his mind. He uses a word to point to the object to which his thought corresponds. When Builder B hears the word, it causes a thought in his mind which corresponds to the same object.

The problem with this explanation is that it doesn't explain why Builder B brings the object to Builder A.

Suppose Builder B is actually a very young girl and Builder A, her father, has to train her for the job. How does he do it? He demonstrates: 'When I say "slab", come to this pile, pick up one of these, and bring it to me over here,' he instructs. 'When I say "beam", come to this pile, pick up one of these, and bring it to me over here.'

Notice that the girl can copy his demonstration without knowing that 'beam' is a name for beams, and so on for the other four words. All she needs to know is that, after her father makes a certain sound, she is supposed to bring him a certain object. In fact, we can easily imagine the father instructing his daughter to bring him a slab when he says 'beam' or when he blows one of four different whistles.

What does this building game tell us?

Meaning as use

It tells us that words get their meaning, not by connecting minds to objects but by being used in activities.

The reason it seems as though words connect minds to objects is because one of the first games we learn to play is the naming game, where an adult points to objects and tells the child the name for it. From this activity we generate the mistaken assumption that the word 'apple' refers to apples.

This assumption is mistaken because it requires us to posit a thought in the mind, an object in the world, and some sort of invisible connection between them. It's much simpler to assert instead that, by copying the examples we see, we learn to associate saying 'apple' with pointing to apples.

In the game of Monopoly, we learn to associate passing 'Go' with collecting $200 (or £200). The game wouldn't work without this rule. Yet 200 Monopoly dollars (or pounds) don't mean anything other than what they allow you to accomplish in the game.

Wittgenstein uses the analogy of games again and again to understand how language works. He goes so far as to assert that language is a game. Games make sense without referring to any reality outside of themselves. Likewise, language works without reference.

Family resemblance

Another significant feature about games is that they are very difficult to define. Usually, defining a term requires identifying what all of its instances have in common. But there isn't anything all games have in common.

The moment you think of a quality that all games have in common, you can always find exceptions. And yet we all easily recognize a game when we see it. How can this be? Wittgenstein addressed this question in his philosophical investigations.

> *Consider for example the proceedings that we call 'games'. I mean board-games, card-games, ball-games, Olympic games, and so on. What is common to them all? – Don't say: 'There must be something common, or they would not be called "games"' – but look and see whether there is anything common to all. – For if you look at them you will not see something that is common to all, but similarities, relationships, and a whole series of them at that. To repeat: don't think, but look!'*
>
> Ludwig Wittgenstein, *Philosophical Investigations*, 66, trans. G.E.M. Anscombe (Oxford: Basil Blackwell, 1958)

Although games don't share a definition, they do share a family resemblance – a series of similarities that establishes a relationship. Biological families provide the primary example of this concept. Consider the Smith family:

▶ The mother has red hair and a big nose.

▶ The father has blond hair and a crooked grin.

▶ The son has red hair and freckles.

▶ The daughter has big nose and a crooked grin.

There is no one quality that all the Smiths share. Yet each shares a quality with at least one of the other members.

Wittgenstein asserts that language is the same way. It consists of a series of interrelated activities, which Wittgenstein calls 'forms of life', such as:

▶ giving and obeying orders

▶ describing or measuring things

▶ reporting on an event

▶ speculating about an event.

While each of these activities shares features with others, there is no one feature common to them all.

Behaviourism

Wittgenstein set out to solve the mystery of how words enable us to connect our thoughts to the world. In the end, he came to the conclusion that they don't. Language is a loosely related set of behaviours that a machine can learn just as well as a human being.

Wittgenstein takes a further, shocking step, however, when he asserts that, because language does not require minds, there is no reason to believe in them.

> *But can't I imagine that the people around me are automata, lack consciousness, even though they behave in the same way as usual? – If I imagine it now – alone in my room – I see people with fixed looks (as in a trance) going about their business – the idea is perhaps a little uncanny. But just try to keep hold of this idea in the midst of your ordinary intercourse with others, in the street, say! Say to yourself, for example: 'The children over there are mere automata; all their liveliness is mere automatism.' And you will either find these words becoming quite meaningless; or you will produce in yourself some kind of uncanny feeling, or something of the sort. Seeing a living human being as an automaton is analogous to seeing one figure as a limiting case or variant of another; the cross-pieces of a window as a swastika, for example.*
>
> Ludwig Wittgenstein, *Philosophical Investigations*, 66, trans. G.E.M. Anscombe (Oxford: Basil Blackwell, 1958)

Wittgenstein presents a thought experiment to motivate this step. Suppose everyone has a small box with a beetle in it. No one is allowed to look in anyone else's box. Instead, we talk about our beetles. Each seems to be a little different from every other. But how do I know you're describing your beetle accurately? Come to think of it, how do I know you have a beetle at all? Does anyone really have a beetle? Perhaps we are all just playing a game.

Likewise, we talk about the thoughts inside our heads, but we never get to see what's really inside. For example, your friend says she believes in God. But this doesn't mean anything unless it makes a difference to what she does – going to church, praying and so forth. If she does nothing different from what she would do if she didn't believe, then her belief may as well not exist.

Suppose you claim you believe in God. Does it make a difference to your behaviour? If not, it's an empty claim. If so, what is the belief other than the behaviour itself?

If we don't need the mind to explain what we do, we should eliminate it. Wittgenstein goes so far as to assert that, for all we know, we are all androids (which he calls 'automata')

We find the swastika creepy only because of its association: we know the history of how it has been used. Likewise, we find the idea of children being androids creepy only because we associate androids with ghosts, aliens and other scary monsters. Without this association, the idea that we are all androids shouldn't be creepy at all.

The view that human life consists in externally observable activities that can be fully understood without reference to any internal, mental states is known as behaviourism. Though Wittgenstein was reluctant to call himself a behaviourist, his view is behaviourist, whether he liked it or not.

He famously asserts: 'One of the most misleading representational techniques in our language is the use of the word "I".'

Perhaps Wittgenstein is right that language creates the illusion of an inner person. On the other hand, without 'I' you couldn't say a lot of things, like 'I love you', which many people – philosophers or not – aren't willing to do without.

Spotlight

Two behaviourists have sex. One turns to the other and says, 'That was good for you: how was it for me?'

Key ideas

Behaviourism: Human life consists of externally observable activities that can be fully understood without reference to any internal subjective states

Conjunction: The logical operation that joins two propositions

Family resemblance: A series of similarities that establishes a relationship among a group of individuals

Formal logic: The systematic study of the relationship between propositions

Negation: The logical operation that denies a proposition

Picture theory of meaning: Wittgenstein's theory that words correspond to the world in the same way pictures do

Reference: The way words connect to the world

Truth table: A method for assigning truth value to complex propositions from their atomic parts

Fact-check

1 Why does the early Wittgenstein reject metaphysics?
 a You can't make a picture of it
 b You can't make a game of it
 c It's useless for architecture
 d It implies we are androids

2 You would use a truth table if you wanted to determine which of the following about a proposition?
 a Whether it is true
 b What all its possible truth values are
 c How it refers to the world
 d Why it is true or false

3 What is Wittgenstein's building game supposed to prove?
 a That children can follow instructions as well as adults
 b That you can't tell whether or not human beings are androids
 c That the meaning of words is a function of how they are used
 d That words correspond to the world in the same way pictures do

4 What did Bertrand Russell's epic failure concern?

 a Marriage

 b Proving 1 + 1 = 2

 c The Nobel Prize in Literature

 d The picture theory of meaning

5 Which of the following is *not* true of language games, according to Wittgenstein?

 a They share family resemblances

 b They can be defined

 c They refer to nothing outside themselves

 d Adults play them just as often as children

6 Which of the following would a behaviourist say?

 a I'm a different person on the inside

 b You can never know how other people really feel

 c Inner happiness is more important than success

 d I am what I do

7 Why does Wittgenstein think 'I' is misleading?

 a Because it suggests someone is 'home'

 b Because we are all interrelated

 c Because self-knowledge is impossible

 d Because it has no logical operation

8 What is the goal of philosophy according to Wittgenstein?

 a Clarification

 b Construction

 c Criticism

 d Creativity

9 Why doesn't Wittgenstein believe in minds?

 a Because they aren't logical

 b Because language doesn't require them

 c Because he found them creepy

 d Because children are often wiser than adults

10 What is 'Wittgenstein's beetle'?

 a A game

 b A picture

 c A machine

 d The mind

Dig deeper

P.M.S. Hacker, *Wittgenstein: Connections and Controversies* (Oxford University Press, 2001)

R.J. Fogelin, *Wittgenstein*, 2nd edn (Routledge & Kegan Paul, 1987)

John Slater, *Bertrand Russell* (Thoemmes Press, 1994)

13

Sartre and existence

'Hell is other people.'
Jean-Paul Sartre

In this chapter you will learn:

▶ *about the problem of human existence*
▶ *the significance of nothingness*
▶ *how bad faith interferes with free will, in Sartre's view*
▶ *the meaning of existentialism*
▶ *how to achieve authenticity, according to Sartre*
▶ *problems with candidates for a fundamental project*
▶ *about de Beauvoir's pioneering contribution to feminism.*

Thought experiment: Mars or Venus?

You're sitting in a large office at the Academy of Intergalactic Exploration. Across a desk full of computer screens, your commander beams at you.

'Good news,' he says, 'everything is ready for your internship. We're sending you to a small planet called Earth. Interesting creatures called humans live there. The only thing left is to decide whether you want us to morph you into a male or a female.

'What do you mean?' you ask.

'Humans come in two types.'

'OK,' you shrug. 'Whichever – it doesn't matter.'

'Oh, but it does,' he insists. 'For starters, males and females have different genitalia. But there are so many ramifications.'

'Like what?'

He raises one finger. 'Males are bigger and stronger on average, which is why male and female athletes compete separately.'

'The males would always tend to win.'

'Right.' He adds a second finger. 'Males also make more money. The statistics vary, but if you go female you're likely to earn about 81 per cent of what you would as a male, and you're not nearly as likely to make it to an executive position.'

'Well, I guess I should go male then...'

'But the males die younger – by a good five years, in most places.' He ticks off a third and fourth finger. 'And they can't have babies.'

'Babies?'

'Yes, human offspring come from the females – right out of their bellies, if you can believe it! – and are highly dependent on them for a long time.'

'Hmm. That sounds like a lot of work.'

'Sure, but there are emotional benefits... Human babies are very cute and cuddly and fun to play with. At any rate, the hormones required for childbearing seem to make females much more sensitive.'

'Being sensitive is liable to make life more difficult, though, isn't it?'

'Perhaps. But females also tend to be more religious, which helps keep them cheerful.'

'Religion could be interesting...'

'Yes, but bear in mind that the religions are run by the males...'

'So the males are usually the executives and the religious authorities...'

'And the government officials.'

'Are they smarter?'

'Apparently not. It's hard to measure. Test scores run about the same. But it's only within the last 100 years or so that the males have started allowing the females to pursue higher education.'

'Sounds like the females are second-class citizens.'

Your commander gazes out the window. 'In ancient times, humans made up two gods, Mars and Venus, who symbolized the difference between the males and the females. Mars is a great warrior and Venus is a great beauty. Which would you rather be?'

You bite your lip. 'I may need a while to think about this.'

Your commander shakes his head. 'We need to morph you now. Don't worry – you can get a sex change there if you come to feel you've made the wrong choice.'

The choice and the given

Have you ever thought about how different your life would be if you were the opposite sex? If you had been given the choice, would you have chosen the sex you are? If it were easy to switch to the opposite sex, would you? Would you be interested in trying it temporarily, just to see what it was like?

Perhaps not, because most people see gender as central to their identity. Take a moment to picture yourself as the opposite sex...

Would you still be you?

Just one little y chromosome – which causes testicle development – makes for the difference. Perhaps, one day, switching will be easy. Perhaps it will become a popular thing to do.

Of those who would switch, do you think more of them would be male switching to female or female switching to male? Why?

Of course, even if you did switch, you would still remember your original gender – the one you grew up with. The 'given' that shaped your life.

Gender is not the only 'given' in your life. You never had the opportunity to choose many things about your identity – the language you speak, your family, the environment around you. And yet, as in the case of gender, you often have much more choice than you think. You can learn a new language, adopt a new family, or move to the other side of the world...

There is a small, unstable space right between the choice and the given. This is where authentic human existence begins, according to the French philosopher Jean-Paul Sartre (1905–80). The most popular philosopher of the twentieth century, Sartre urges us to find this space to escape the problem of human existence.

The problem of human existence

After being taken prisoner of war by the Nazis, and reading Heidegger (whom we met in Chapter 11) during his confinement, Sartre became concerned about the problem of human existence. He felt that the entire history of philosophy had failed to show that there was anything special or important about being human.

In fact, insofar as we see the history of philosophy culminating in Wittgenstein, we're liable to walk away from it utterly depressed. Perhaps there isn't anything special or important about being human. Perhaps we are all organic androids.

Or perhaps things got off track. How did we come to see ourselves in such a limited way? Sartre pinpoints the problem in science. When empiricism overtook innatism, banishing the supernatural outlook on the work, intellectuals became giddy with the power of the scientific method. They came to believe that it could explain everything, including human existence.

But science also helped to produce two world wars during Sartre's lifetime. Witnessing their ravages first hand, Sartre came to believe that science has its limits. Heidegger's great insight, in Sartre's view, was to reject the objectifying metaphysics of Western philosophy in favour of a subjective ontology which would allow for a richer description of reality. Yet Heidegger's obsession with the effort to conceptualize being itself left him without enough insight into the particular human way of being.

Sartre was a keen observer of humanity. He loved nothing more than to sit at a café, smoke a cigarette, and watch what people do. It's no wonder that he won a Nobel Prize in Literature for his many novels and plays. He wove a great deal of literary description into his philosophical works as well. One of the things he noticed while people-watching became the key to his solution to the problem of human existence.

Nothingness

You arrive at the café expecting to meet your friend Pierre. You push through the door, perhaps a bit flushed and out of breath from your effort to be there on time. Your eyes are bright and expectant. You scan the room...

No Pierre.

Your face changes. You scan the room again, your eyes searching. They are seeing, not what is in the room, but a void in the shape of your friend.

Pierre is not there.

It is a simple fact. We can state it objectively and analyse its logic. Let P = the proposition 'Pierre is there.' Then what you have discovered is:

$$\neg P$$

This proposition is logically equivalent to:

¬R

where R = the proposition 'Roger is not there' and so on for a thousand other propositions just like it.

And yet it's not the same at all.

When you arrived at the café, you experienced Pierre's absence. You didn't experience the absence of Roger or anyone else. But Pierre's void was tangible. Sartre goes so far as to assert that it 'haunted' you.

Everyone has experienced the absence of something. According to Sartre, this common experience is evidence that the logic of objective, scientific description is inadequate. For humans, there are not just objects in the world, but also their absences. There is being, and there is nothingness. The discovery of nothingness is crucial because it gives us free will.

Spotlight

Sartre is sitting in a café writing in a notebook about nothingness.

A waitress approaches him, saying, 'Can I get you something to drink, Monsieur Sartre?'

'Yes,' he replies. 'I'd like a cup of coffee with sugar, but no cream.'

Nodding agreement, the waitress walks off to fill the order and Sartre resumes writing. A few minutes later, however, the waitress returns and says:

'I'm sorry, Monsieur Sartre, we are out of cream – how about with no milk?'

Free will

The scientific world view championed by empiricist philosophers leads to the conclusion that free choice is an illusion. For example, Thomas Hobbes, whom we met in Chapter 6, argues that human beings are just animals driven by animal desires. Although our advanced intelligence makes it seem as though we make choices, in reality the strongest desire always determines what we do.

Sartre rejects this determinist outlook, which he thinks is produced by focusing only on what exists. By focusing on nothingness, we discover that non-being is the birthplace of possibility.

Right now you are reading this book. Stop for a moment and think of yourself getting up and throwing the book out of the window ...

Because this version of you doesn't exist, it is pure nothingness. Although you can't experience something that doesn't exist, you can experience the void it creates.

There are two possible versions of you: the one that goes on reading this book and the one that gets up and throws the book out of the window. Both are pure nothing, and therefore both are genuine possibilities for you.

Awareness of nothingness is a state of mind. You have to notice the things you are not in order to realize you are free. The problem is that most people most of the time avoid this realization because they are mired in bad faith.

Bad faith

Going back to the café scenario where you hoped to meet Pierre, Sartre describes the waiter. He comes to your table and greets you with an eager speech he has given a thousand times. His movements are so efficient that they are mechanical. He smiles considerately without ever quite looking you in the eye. He is playing his role. He has turned himself off. He doesn't want to think or feel anything because his job doesn't allow it.

Sartre argues that most of us spend much more time acting like the waiter than we would like to admit. We find ourselves in rigidly defined social roles: student, parent, spouse, employee and so on. In order to carry out these roles day in and day out, we become passively detached, ignoring all the possibilities free will presents to us.

Sartre calls this way of living **bad faith**. Although the waiter is trying to forget that he is free, he nevertheless freely chose to allow himself to descend into this disenchanted state. He is therefore responsible for what has happened to him. Moreover, he still catches a glimpse, from time to time, of what he has become. He is engaged in an elaborate form of self-deception.

Looked at one way, the waiter is disciplined – a true professional. Looked at another way, he has lost his humanity. By refusing to engage with the world subjectively, he has become an object in the world – a mere thing.

> *A grocer who dreams is offensive to the buyer, because such a grocer is not wholly a grocer. Society demands that he limit himself to his function as a grocer, just as the soldier at attention makes himself into a soldier-thing with a direct regard which does not see at all, which is no longer meant to see, since it is the rule and not the interest of the moment which determines the point he must fix his eyes on (the sight 'fixed at ten paces'). There are indeed many precautions to imprison a man in what he is, as if we lived in perpetual fear that he might escape from it, that he might break away and suddenly elude his condition.*
>
> Jean-Paul Sartre, *Being and Nothingness*, trans. Hazel E. Barnes (New York: Simon & Schuster, 1992), p. 102.

The waiter, the grocer and you may as well be androids. While Wittgenstein is content to accept this, Sartre is not.

Sartre calls a mere object in the world a **being-in-itself**. A chair, a cat and an android – each of these is a being-in-itself. You, on the other hand, have the potential to become a **being-for-itself**: a conscious subject that defines itself by making choices.

Existentialism

Self-definition is the task we must all undertake in order to realize our potential, according to Sartre. He places self-definition at the centre of his philosophy, which he calls **existentialism**.

Traditionally, philosophers see it as an important part of their job to define things by identifying their essence. For example, it is the essence of a cup to hold liquid. Needless to say, the definition of humanity has always been hotly debated. Existentialists go so far as to deny that humanity can be defined, asserting that, in our case, existence precedes essence.

What do we mean by saying that existence precedes essence? We mean that man first of all exists, encounters himself, surges up in the world – and defines himself afterwards. If man as the existentialist sees him is not definable, it is because to begin with he is nothing. He will not be anything until later, and then he will be what he makes of himself. Thus, there is no human nature, because there is no God to have a conception of it. Man simply is. Not that he is simply what he conceives himself to be, but he is what he wills, and as he conceives himself after already existing – as he wills to be after that leap towards existence. Man is nothing else but that which he makes of himself. That is the first principle of existentialism.

Jean-Paul Sartre, *Existentialism Is a Humanism* (http://www.marxists.org/reference/archive/sartre/works/exist/sartre.htm)

The possibilities that free will presents cannot be limited.

Granted, everyone is born with a set of 'givens' – gender, language, family, environment. Sartre calls this the 'facticity' that each individual must transcend. If you are a female in a Spanish-speaking family in Southern California, then you must either willingly embrace this identity or willingly change it. As Sartre puts it, freedom is what you do with what's been done to you.

Whether you willingly embrace what you have or willingly change it, the wilful element makes your new identity authentic. Authenticity is the antidote to bad faith. It means having the courage to follow your passion, breaking out of imposed social roles to be true to yourself.

But how does one go about accomplishing this?

The fundamental project

Because authenticity is an expression of radical freedom, existentialism cannot specify how to achieve it. Existentialists focus, not so much on what you do, but how you do it. You could wait tables authentically if this was part of your fundamental project.

For Sartre, a fundamental project is a long-term commitment that begins with a free choice, giving unity and meaning to your subsequent actions. It becomes the ultimate reason for virtually everything you do.

It's easy to think of projects that aren't fundamental, such as fixing the garage door, training for a marathon or planning a holiday. These are temporary pastimes that have little lasting impact on your identity as a person.

The fundamental project transcends the trivial concerns of daily life. Sartre describes it as an abstract desire for pure being that transforms you. There are three main candidates for the fundamental project, each of which comes with its own difficulties.

First candidate: relationships

Sartre had a lifelong love affair with Simone de Beauvoir (1908–96), who was a philosopher in her own right. Their relationship was famously stormy, unconventional and controversial.

Falling in love may not exactly be a choice, but it is your choice whether or not to pursue the relationship. In a relationship, you want to become something new by uniting with the other in mind and body. The other has to be just as radically free as you are in order for you to create a partnership of mutual desire.

The problem is that radical freedom makes the unity inherently unstable. The effort to stabilize it turns desire into possessiveness and control, which in turn undermines freedom. The other person becomes the 'Other': an objectified subject.

Sartre and de Beauvoir tried to pursue their relationship creatively. They never married and never had children. They allowed each other to have affairs and often included others in their sexual relations. In fact, they seduced their own teenage students, many of whom apparently suffered emotional damage, including suicide in one case. Perhaps it would be possible for love to be the answer for an existentialist, but it was not for Sartre.

Second candidate: political activism

After he was released from the Nazi prison camp, Sartre joined the French Resistance, publishing subversive tracts and contributing to the subsequent peace movement in many ways.

Because authenticity is based on radical freedom, the question arises whether Nazism – Hitler's bid to take over the world – could constitute a fundamental project. In a popular lecture he gave concerning the basic tenets of existentialism, Sartre argues no. An unethical project can never be authentic because it is destructive of, rather than desirous of, pure being. Harking back to Kant (whom we met in Chapter 9), Sartre claims that a truly authentic project must somehow be universalizable – the kind of thing one could consistently will everyone to will.

Sartre later renounced this lecture, however, saying it was the only work he ever regretted publishing. Critics charge that Sartre's belated and half-hearted interest in duty contradicts his original claim that individuals define themselves from pure nothing. They also criticize his political activism as opportunist and self-serving. Perhaps it would be possible for political activism to be the answer for an existentialist, but not for Sartre.

Third candidate: art

Sartre seems to have found his greatest fulfilment in life through his novels and plays, which were instant sensations and have become world classics. Ten thousand people turned out on the streets of Paris on the day he died in 1980 – a testament to his ability to touch people's hearts as an artist.

Sartre asserts that one of the chief motives for artistic creation is the need to feel that we are essential to the world. Existentialism encourages individuals to define themselves, and art is a vehicle for expressing that individuality. It connects us to other human beings so that we aren't alone in our freedom.

Yet Sartre was ambivalent about this connection. Though he was awarded the Nobel Prize in Literature, he became the first ever to reject it (along with its cash reward). He called it too 'bourgeois' – referring to the middle class, which existentialists have long criticized as a class of mediocre people devoted to material gain. In the end, Sartre hid from his adoring fans and became addicted to amphetamines. So, evidently, art was not the answer for him either.

Spotlight

Despite its enthusiastic celebration of human freedom, there is a dark side to existentialism. Sartre memorably quipped that we are 'condemned to be free'. While freedom is intoxicating, it also produces the overwhelming sense of responsibility that Sartre calls **nausea**. You cannot blame anyone else for what you become. And, as it turns out, it's not at all easy to become something good.

Case study: Simone de Beauvoir and feminism

Throughout Western history women have been denied the respect and leisure time required to make important intellectual contributions. Towards the end of the twentieth century, when women were finally allowed to pursue higher education, they began to appear in all academic areas, including philosophy. Simone de Beauvoir, Sartre's lifelong partner, became one of the first female philosophers. She was also a strong proponent of feminism, the movement defending equal rights for women.

De Beauvoir's most important work is a two-volume treatise called *The Second Sex* (1949). In it, de Beauvoir analyses the status of women as second-class citizens in Western culture. She writes:

> One is not born, but rather becomes, a woman. No biological, psychological, or economic fate determines the figure that the human female presents in society; it is civilization as a whole that produces this creature, intermediate between male and eunuch, which is described as feminine. Only the intervention of someone else can establish an individual as Other. [...] If, well before puberty and sometimes even from early infancy, she seems to us to be already sexually determined, this is not because mysterious instincts directly doom her to passivity, coquetry, maternity; it is

because the influence of others upon the child is a factor almost from the start, and thus she is indoctrinated with her vocation from her earliest years.

Simone de Beauvoir, *The Second Sex*, trans. H.M. Parshley (New York: Penguin, 1972), pp. 273–4 (http://hagocrat.files.wordpress.com/2012/06/de-beauvoir-simone-second-sex.pdf)

The vocation of the female is to serve the male, and this is something that must change.

De Beauvoir further developed Sartre's existentialism, applying it more specifically to the female point of view. Patiently collecting and editing Sartre's work, she was a constant inspiration for him, even after they ceased to be lovers. As in the case of John Stuart Mill's partner, Harriet Taylor, some give de Beauvoir credit as Sartre's unacknowledged co-author.

Feminists would insist that the situation of Taylor and de Beauvoir was not at all unusual because, behind every great man, there is a great woman.

Key ideas

Authenticity: having the courage to follow your passion, breaking out of imposed social roles to be true to yourself
Bad faith: Living in denial of freedom
Being-in-itself: A non-conscious object in the world
Being-for-itself: A conscious subject that defines itself by making choices
Existentialism: The view that human beings must define themselves
Facticity: The set of givens that each person is born with
Fundamental project: A long-term commitment that begins with a free choice, giving unity and meaning to your subsequent actions
Feminism: The movement defending equal rights for women
Nausea: The overwhelming sense of responsibility freedom produces
Nothingness: The lack of being that gives us free will
The Other: The other person as objectified subject in a relationship

Fact-check

1 Sartre famously wrote: 'Hell is other people.' To which of the following is this most likely to refer?
   a The problem of divine punishment
   b The problem of the objectified subject
   c The problem of nothingness
   d The problem of bourgeois authenticity

2 Sartre argues that freedom arises from which of the following?
   a Nothing
   b Everything
   c Inner peace
   d People-watching

3 According to Sartre, an android is which of the following?
   a A being-for-itself
   b A being-in-itself
   c A non-existing being
   d A desire for pure being

4 Which of the following is an example of facticity?
   a A sex change
   b True love
   c Music
   d A big nose

5 Which of the following would Sartre consider a candidate for the fundamental project?
   a Establishing a feminist co-operative
   b Buying a pet
   c Earning a college degree
   d Starting a business

6 Authenticity involves which of the following for Sartre?
   a Loving others as you love yourself
   b Discovering your innate essence
   c Following God's plan
   d Breaking out of social roles

7 Which of the following promotes bad faith, according to Sartre?
   a Authenticity
   b Art
   c Atheism
   d Social roles

8 Why does de Beauvoir say that one is not born a woman?
   a Because being a woman is a vocation imposed by society
   b Because babies are essentially asexual
   c Because the distinction between male and female is arbitrary
   d Because not all women deserve to be considered women

9 Which of the following could be an expression of nausea?
   a I did this
   b I want to do this
   c I hope this will happen
   d What happened?

10 Which of the following corrupted the history of philosophy, according to Sartre?
   a Art
   b Political activism
   c Science
   d Women

Dig deeper

N. Bauer, *Simone de Beauvoir, Philosophy, and Feminism* (Columbia University Press, 2001)

A.C. Danto, *Sartre* (Fontana, 1991)

Adrian Van den Hoven and Andrew Leak, eds, *Sartre Today: A Centenary Celebration* (Berghahn Books, 2005)

Dewey and truth

'We think only when we are confronted with problems.'

John Dewey

In this chapter you will learn:

▶ *the difference between aesthetic realism and expressionism*

▶ *the connection between beauty and truth, according to Dewey*

▶ *why Dewey sees language as a tool*

▶ *the meaning of the claim that truth is what works*

▶ *about the pragmatist view of knowledge*

▶ *how Hegel influenced Dewey and Marx in different ways*

▶ *about the progressive view of learning.*

Thought experiment: the egg

You are taking a long walk along the beach at sunset. The ocean breeze plays mischievously with your hair. Waves crash against your feet. Pink and orange clouds glide across the horizon.

You walk for a long time – out to a majestic old pier and then back to where you left your picnic blanket. When you arrive, it's dark, but the moon casts a silver light across the sand.

Startled, you catch sight of something you've never seen before sitting near your picnic blanket.

As you stare at it, chills run down your spine.

You approach slowly, glancing around to see whether someone else is on the beach. There's no one as far as the eye can see.

You bend to pick up the object. It appears to be an elaborately carved piece of driftwood. It must have been a fat stump at one time, you conjecture, judging by the width of the wood, but it's largely hollow inside and surprisingly light. Smooth tendrils wind around the surface to form an oval – like a giant Easter egg.

You look around again, wondering how it arrived at your blanket. Did it wash up in the tide? Did the wind blow it across the sand?

You hear a noise behind you and turn to see two large seagulls fighting over a dead fish. Could an animal have dragged the driftwood to this place?

Surely not. Surely someone made it and left it here.

But is it for you? Should you take it? After debating in your mind for a while and looking around again in vain for other people, you decide you can't bear to leave such a beautiful object to its possible demise.

Still baffled the next day, you bring it to three different kinds of expert: a naturalist, a historian and an artist. Each comes to a different conclusion.

The naturalist pronounces that the object is the remains of a large nest made by gribbles – marine worms that decompose wood. A pattern of marks along the edges of the tendrils show the paths along which they burrowed into the wood and made ventilation holes.

The historian disagrees. In ancient times, Vikings threw wood into the sea to determine the best place to land their ships. The tiny holes in this ingenious buoy show where a craftsman used needle and thread to attach a flag to the wood so that it would be more visible from a distance.

The artist shakes her head at both of these proposals. The markings on the wood are deliberately arranged in a geometrical pattern suggestive of a neo-pagan nature motif. The sculpture is a very talented artist's symbolic representation of new life.

You take your 'egg' back home and place it at the centre of the dining-room table. You enjoy looking at it. Everyone who sees it admires it. It doesn't seem to matter who made it – gribbles, Vikings or a professional sculptor – it is an inspiration to you.

Then one day it disappears just as suddenly as it appeared.

The secret of learning

The above thought experiment was originally suggested by the American philosopher John Dewey (1859–1952). Dewey is considered the most influential American philosopher of the twentieth century because he developed a daringly original point of view and pursued its implications outside academia – in the political and social arena.

The driving concern of Dewey's career was how people learn. He proposed educational reforms that reverberate today throughout schools worldwide.

Most people have had enough bad experiences with school to know that learning isn't something that just magically happens when a teacher wants it to. In fact, for some people, the very word 'learning' means 'suffering through infinite boredom while some tyrannical authority figure tries to get you to care about something stupid and irrelevant'. This attitude is all too common, and it worried Dewey.

Dewey was convinced that learning is not just about school –
it's a lifelong process, the only process through which human
beings can truly grow and flourish. If you've ever had a positive
learning experience – at school or elsewhere – then you know
that there is nothing quite so satisfying and rewarding. What's
the secret of these experiences? Dewey was determined to figure
it out. His investigation begins with art.

Spotlight

Dewey was the classic absent-minded professor. He is reported to
have walked to the post office with his infant son in a pushchair.
Upon receiving an interesting-looking envelope, he left the child in
his pushchair and read the letter all the way home.

Art

What is art? You know it when you see it, but it's not an easy
thing to define.

Aesthetics is the branch of philosophy that studies the nature of
art. There are many different aesthetic theories. Dewey's is best
understood against the most traditional theory, which is known
as **aesthetic realism**.

According to realists, the purpose of art is to create an accurate
representation of reality. A good painting, on this view, is one
that looks like a photograph. A good play is one that recreates a
series of events that actually happened or could have happened,
without relying on artificial or imaginary devices.

Aesthetic realism is commonly assumed to be the only standard
by which art can be judged. When you compliment a child for
placing two eyes in the right place on his self-portrait, you're
assuming that the child's goal is (or should be) to make the
picture look as similar to himself as possible. Likewise, when
you complain that a novel had an 'implausible ending', you're
assuming that a good story should mimic real life.

Dewey would challenge your realist assumption in each case,
advancing an **expressionist** alternative. According to expressionism,

art is an outpouring of inner experience. A child may draw his self-portrait without eyes because he is thinking about some things he saw recently that scared him. Likewise, if a novel is really about what the author was thinking and feeling, then it is appropriate for it to have an imaginative rather than a realistic ending.

For Dewey, art originates with the need to communicate our deepest thoughts and feelings, many of which are subconscious – meaning that that we are not directly aware of them. Everyone has this need, and hence everyone is potentially an artist. In fact, Dewey asserts that a great deal of unhappiness in the world results from pent-up emotions.

But not just any emotional discharge makes for a successful work of art. A successful work of art releases inner meaning through a medium in a way that restores harmony and can be appreciated by others. While professional artists may be especially admired, everyone should strive for an artistic outlet, and art should be a regular omnipresent aspect of life, rather than a dusty old thing in a museum.

For Dewey, the 'egg' you found in the thought experiment at the opening of this chapter is especially intriguing because you don't know whether it even has a meaning, much less what that meaning is. Aesthetic appreciation of the object would involve positing an artist and speculating on their intentions – relating to them based on one's own inner experience.

But what if you found out that the object was a Viking buoy?

I found I could say things with color and shapes that I couldn't say any other way ... things I had no words for.
Georgia O'Keeffe

Technology

Tools, machines and other things humans invent to solve problems are called technology, from the Greek word for 'craft'. Dewey doesn't want to make much of a distinction between art and technology insofar as each is the solution to a problem.

While art solves an internal problem, technology solves an external one. Vikings made buoys because they needed to know where to land their ships. Driftwood laced with a flag creates a visible marker along the path of least resistance. Human beings have invented countless technologies like this, from the simplest wheel to the most advanced computer.

If technologies are tools for solving problems, however, then they need not always be physical objects. A simple pencil is technology because it is a tool for communicating. And if a pencil is a technology, then so is a spoken word. Dewey argues that language is the ultimate tool of tools, because it has the power to co-ordinate the efforts of many people in solving problems.

Hence, words and pictures can equally be considered art or technology – the distinction becomes arbitrary by virtue of the common problem-solving nature of each. In fact, Dewey warns against strict categories that make distinctions where none exist. He is especially critical of the dualist's distinction between mind and body, as proposed by Descartes, whom we met in Chapter 5.

Dewey goes so far as to assert that the institutions created by words and pictures – including religion, science and politics – are technologies. We can admire or despise them just like any work of art. The most important thing to keep in mind is that they are human inventions, created, like a buoy, to solve particular problems.

If an institution creates more problems than it solves, then it has outlived its usefulness and must be replaced, according to Dewey. He is especially critical of religion on the grounds that it creates divisions among people, to the point of war in many cases. He argues that the 'spiritual' experiences that religion celebrates can be accepted as real without being designated 'supernatural'. For Dewey, nature is rich and deep enough to account for even the most transcendent phenomena.

Nature

Dewey was a strong supporter of Charles Darwin's theory of natural selection, which we discussed in Chapter 4. He was also a great defender of science in general. But his view of science is much broader than the traditional view criticized by Sartre in Chapter 13.

Go back to the 'egg' you found in our thought experiment. Suppose it turns out to be the product of marine worms after all. Then it isn't art and it isn't technology, but it is still a valuable source of inspiration. Dewey argues that science has not solved all the mysteries in nature. Although the empirical method enables us to measure and predict many things, it also discovers intangible beauty and the goodness it implies.

If experience actually presents aesthetic and moral traits, then these traits may also be supposed to reach down into nature, and to testify to something that belongs to nature as truly as does the mechanical structure attributed to it in physical science. To rule out that possibility by some general reasoning is to forget that the very meaning and purport of empirical method is that things are to be studied on their own account, so as to find out what is revealed when they are experienced. The traits possessed by the subject-matters of experience are as genuine as the characteristics of sun and electron. They are found, experienced, and are not to be shoved out of being by some trick of logic.

John Dewey, *Experience and Nature* (1925) (http://www.scienzepostmoderne.org/OpereComplete/Dewey.John..Experience%20and%20Nature%20%281925,%201929%29pdf)

Beauty is not a figment of our imagination – an interpretation we arbitrarily impose on the world. It is a type of experience just as real as any other truth. The catch, according to Dewey, is that, just as there is no absolute beauty, there is no absolute truth.

Truth

Recall that, according to aesthetic realism, the purpose of art is to create an accurate representation of reality. A picture is good insofar as it reflects its subject matter like a photograph. Although this view is commonly assumed, we have seen why Dewey rejects it.

As it turns out, realism is also the most common theory of the nature of truth. Realism about truth (also called **correspondence theory**) holds that a statement can be called 'true' precisely insofar as it accurately represents reality.

At first, this view seems so obvious that it must be indisputable. There is a cat on the mat. I assert: 'The cat is on the mat.' My statement is true because it mirrors exactly what is the case. How could anyone think truth is anything different?

On closer examination, however, we see that this question is like asking, 'How could anyone think it OK for someone with eyes to draw a self-portrait without eyes? Such a picture does not correspond to the reality, and so it must be wrong.'

We've seen how expressionism challenges this way of thinking. If the purpose of art is to solve an emotional problem, then a self-portrait without eyes might be exactly right. It might even be beautiful if it is experienced as such by the artist and the viewer. While this beauty may be a real experience for the people involved, it isn't absolute because it may not affect other people the same way. The portrait is a tool that is emotionally effective for certain people at certain times.

In a parallel way, factual statements are tools used to solve intellectual problems. To the extent that they are successful, we call them 'true'. If I assert that the cat is on the mat, and someone else finds evidence indicating that the cat is not on the mat, then my statement is still problematic. Its truth is in doubt. If, on the other hand, my statement enables me to accomplish something – let's say my telling you where the cat is enables you to catch it in order to remove it from the house – then it worked for our purposes, and we may call it true.

To suppose there is something more to truth than what works is to suppose there is some godlike figure who can compare bare statements to bare reality without any purposes in mind. But there is no such objective point of view. Every point of view has a purpose and truths are statements that help to carry them out.

Pragmatism

Dewey was one of the founders of the school of thought known as **pragmatism** (from the Greek word for 'practical'), a naturalistic epistemology that views knowledge as the solution to practical problems. This view is 'naturalistic' because it conceives of human beings as biological organisms struggling to survive.

If you moved through the world effortlessly, accomplishing all your goals without a single challenge, you would never acquire knowledge. Picture a ball of tumbleweed tumbling across the desert. It goes wherever the wind blows – it stops, it changes course, it tumbles on. Because it has no goals, it has no problems; because it has no problems, it doesn't need to know anything.

You, however, are a very different story. You have a lot of goals, from the simplest desire to eat food to the most sophisticated plan to save the planet. You constantly encounter obstacles. To get food, you need to get money; to get money, you need to hold down a job; to hold down a job, you need to arrive on time. But heavy traffic during morning rush hour keeps making you late regardless of which roads you drive. So you learn to take the train.

You learn.

According to Dewey, knowledge is something you learn through experience as opposed to just repeating or nodding agreement.

Suppose your parents had always tried to teach you that the train is a superior mode of transport. This information is meaningless to you until you find out for yourself. And it may not hold true for everyone all the time.

According to pragmatists, knowledge arises from a process that starts with an obstacle to successful human action, proceeds to active manipulation of the environment to test hypotheses, and issues in a change that allows for the action to proceed once again.

Scepticism: the mark and even the pose of the educated mind.
John Dewey

Realists object that pragmatists mistake one type of knowledge – practical knowledge – for knowledge itself. Surely, there are many kinds of knowledge that don't fit the pragmatist formula. For example: the Nazis killed millions of Jews during World War II. This is a historical claim. It seems important to know whether it corresponds to reality.

In response to this objection, Dewey would insist that pragmatism can make perfect sense of the truth about the Nazis. While he would debunk the study of history for history's sake, he would insist that history is a science and is therefore subject to the same rigorous standards as any other science.

> *If a scientific man be asked what is truth, he will reply – if he frame his reply in terms of his practice and not of some convention – that which is accepted upon adequate evidence. And if he is asked for a description of adequacy of evidence, he certainly will refer to matters of observation and experiment. It is not the self-inclosed character of the terms and propositions nor their systematic ordering which settles the case for him; it is the way they were obtained and what he can do with them in getting other things.*
>
> John Dewey, *Essays in Experimental Logic* (http://www.gutenberg.org/files/40794/40794-h/40794-h.htm)

Genghis Khan also slaughtered millions of people. This truth is less certain and less important than the one about the Nazis because of the latter's ongoing impact on our lives. Holocaust survivors remain and there will be living memory of World War II for a very long time.

The truths of history, like the truths of all the traditional academic subjects, are important insofar as they are practical, and they are practical insofar as they are part of our daily lives. Gaining knowledge of these truths helps solve the most important problem human beings face – namely, how to maintain a civil society. This highly complex endeavour requires the noble enterprise known as education.

Case study: Marx and historical progress

Dewey was strongly influenced by the early nineteenth-century German philosopher G.W.F. Hegel (1770–1831), an idealist like Plato, whom we met in Chapter 1. Hegel's belief in an ideal realm beyond the world of sense experience led him to posit the existence of an absolute spirit of pure reason that guides the progress of history.

While rejecting Hegel's idealism, Dewey remained convinced that the collective use of reason can bring about the gradual and continual improvement of society. His optimism pervades his philosophy and is sometimes criticized as naive ignorance of underlying problems.

The nineteenth-century German philosopher Karl Marx was also strongly influenced by Hegel's notion of the inevitable progress of history. Marx was not as optimistic as Dewey, however. He identified major societal problems stemming from capitalism, the free-market economic system of the Western world.

Capitalism requires the existence of private property. Those with wealth (the 'ruling class') own businesses and hire workers ('proletarians') to make products to sell. Because each product has competitors, it has to be priced as low as possible. This means making the workplace maximally efficient and paying the workers as little as possible, making them miserable.

Marx advocates replacing capitalism with communism, a co-operative system that would eliminate private property so that wealth and control of production could be shared equally among everyone. According to Marx's analysis, the history of civilization is passing through five progressive stages, the last of which will involve a communist revolution. He writes:

> *Let the ruling classes tremble at a communist revolution. The proletarians have nothing to lose but their chains. They have a world to win. Workingmen of all countries, unite!*
>
> Karl Marx, *The Communist Manifesto*, Ch. 4 (http://www.marxists.org/archive/marx/works/1848/communist-manifesto/ch04htm)

Marx's works have ignited powerful social movements and influenced politics around the world.

Education

Applying pragmatism to education produced the school of thought known as **progressivism**. Making significant impact on schools around the world throughout the latter half of the twentieth century, progressives reject the traditional approach to learning through information-imparting and testing in favour of interactive, problem-solving projects relevant to daily life.

Dewey tested the viability of his progressive ideals by establishing a laboratory school at the University of Chicago. His students there studied chemistry, not by memorizing formulas but by baking biscuits. They studied geometry, not by deducing axioms, but by making patterns to sew their own clothes. He wanted them to rely on each other for information and ideas: to form a **community of inquirers**. Dewey's laboratory school still exists. Although its success is controversial, it continues to provide a model for innovative teachers.

Dewey argues that education is a process of living, not a preparation for future living. Because life is problem-solving and problem-solving is learning, learning should extend far beyond the classroom.

Dewey embraced the liberal political views advanced by John Locke, whom we met in Chapter 7. He was convinced that democracy could achieve the liberal ideals of freedom and equality, but only to the extent that its members conceived of themselves as active truth-seekers for whom every problem is an opportunity for growth.

Key ideas

Aesthetics: The branch of philosophy that studies the nature of art

Aesthetic realism: The view that the purpose of art is to create an accurate representation of reality

Capitalism: The free-market economic system of the Western world

Communism: A co-operative economic system that eliminates private property so that wealth and control of production can be shared equally among everyone

Correspondence theory (realism about truth): The view that a statement can be called 'true' precisely insofar as it accurately represents reality

Expressionism: The view that art is an outpouring of inner experience

Technology: Tools, machines and other things humans invent to solve problems

Pragmatism: A naturalistic epistemology that views knowledge as the solution to practical problems

Progressivism (educational): Rejection of traditional information-imparting and testing in favour of interactive, problem-solving projects relevant to daily life

Fact-check

1 An aesthetic realist is most likely to prefer which of the following?

   a   Songs from the Beatles' LSD period

   b   A discordant symphony

   c   An opera about trolls and garden fairies

   d   A concerto that reproduces various bird calls

2 Which of the following adjectives would be the most likely for describing an expressionist painting?

   a   Angry

   b   Realistic

   c   Accurate

   d   Photographic

3 Which of the following is *not* a tool, according to Dewey?

   a   Universities

   b   Computers

   c   An apartment building

   d   A beaver dam

4 Which of the following lesson plans would Dewey be most likely to recommend?

   a   Reading about the causes of inner-city poverty

   b   Working at an inner-city soup kitchen

   c   Reading a novel about a family living in the inner city

   d   Attending a lecture about poverty by a professor who grew up in the inner city

5 Why did Marx think it necessary to eliminate private property?

   a   Because collective reasoning must occur in public

   b   To maximize productivity in the workplace

   c   Because corruption occurs more easily behind closed doors

   d   So that wealth and control of production could be shared equally among everyone

6 Which of the following would be a good reason for studying sociology, according to Dewey?

   a   To get a good job

   b   To pass knowledge to the next generation

   c To solve social problems

   d For fun

7 What is truth, according to Dewey?

   a A statement that works

   b A statement that corresponds to reality

   c A statement of absolute spirit

   d A statement of expression

8 Which of the following is most likely to be an instance of true learning, in Dewey's view?

   a You finally untangled the knot in your shoelaces

   b You memorized the multiplication table

   c You sent a belated birthday card to a friend

   d You read Shakespeare

9 In which of the following ways does Dewey think beauty is like truth?

   a Both are dangerous

   b Neither is absolute

   c Both are an expression of absolute spirit

   d Neither is attained through the use of reason

10 Which of the following is the most accurate description of Dewey?

   a Revolutionary

   b Reformer

   c Conservative

   d Reactionary

Dig deeper

James Campbell, *Understanding John Dewey: Nature and Cooperative Intelligence* (Open Court, 1995)

Larry A. Hickman, *John Dewey's Pragmatic Technology* (Indiana University Press, 1990)

Philip W. Jackson, *John Dewey and the Lessons of Art* (Yale University Press, 1998)

Afterword

The most enduring questions human beings have ever asked arise through the topics we covered in this book:

- Justice
- Friendship
- God
- The Soul
- Freedom
- Knowledge
- Causality

- Duty
- Happiness
- Meaning
- Language
- Existence
- Truth

The philosophers who tackled these topics have guided the development of Western civilization. Their ideas trickle down to all of us through contemporary culture, whether we are aware of it or not.

Beyond its importance on a historical and societal level, philosophy speaks to each of us on a personal level. We all have to work out how to live. This single question lies at the bottom of all philosophical investigation. By standing on philosophers' shoulders, we gain the courage to challenge the assumptions that keep us from becoming the people we want to be.

Our survey of the greatest philosophers of Western history ends in the twentieth century. It remains to be seen what will be the most important philosophy of the twenty-first century and where it will take us.

Answers

CHAPTER 1	CHAPTER 3	CHAPTER 5	CHAPTER 7
1 d	1 d	1 b	1 b
2 b	2 a	2 b	2 a
3 b	3 a	3 a	3 d
4 a	4 d	4 c	4 d
5 a	5 b	5 d	5 a
6 a	6 a	6 b	6 a
7 b	7 b	7 c	7 b
8 a	8 b	8 a	8 c
9 d	9 c	9 c	9 a
10 c	10 c	10 a	10 a

CHAPTER 2	CHAPTER 4	CHAPTER 6	CHAPTER 8
1 b	1 b	1 b	1 b
2 c	2 a	2 a	2 a
3 d	3 d	3 b	3 b
4 a	4 a	4 d	4 b
5 b	5 b	5 d	5 d
6 a	6 d	6 c	6 a
7 a	7 b	7 b	7 a
8 d	8 b	8 b	8 d
9 d	9 d	9 c	9 d
10 d	10 c	10 a	10 c

CHAPTER 9	CHAPTER 11	CHAPTER 13
1 d	1 b	1 b
2 b	2 b	2 a
3 a	3 d	3 b
4 a	4 d	4 d
5 b	5 b	5 a
6 a	6 c	6 d
7 b	7 a	7 d
8 c	8 a	8 a
9 d	9 a	9 a
10 b	10 b	10 c

CHAPTER 10	CHAPTER 12	CHAPTER 14
1 b	1 a	1 d
2 b	2 b	2 a
3 a	3 c	3 d
4 d	4 b	4 b
5 d	5 b	5 d
6 d	6 d	6 c
7 b	7 a	7 a
8 c	8 a	8 a
9 a	9 b	9 b
10 a	10 d	10 b

Index